NAMMET

A CELEBRATION OF ISLE OF WIGHT FOOD AND DRINK

Orchard Bay

Arreton Valley

Nammet

Published by
Medina Publishing Ltd
310 Ewell Road
Surbiton
Surrey KT6 7AL
medinapublishing.com

Photographs © Julian Winslow, Cam Snudden and Steve Gasgoigne 2018
Text © Earl Mountbatten Hospice 2018

Designed by Fred Smith
Edited by Caroline Gurney-Champion

ISBN 978-1-911487-08-1

British Library Cataloguing-in-Publication Data
A catalogue record for this publication is available from the British Library

Printed and bound by Oriental Press, Dubai

Cover photo: Robert Thompson, award-winning patron chef of Thompson's Restaurant,
Newport, Isle of Wight. Robert looks no further than the producers outside his front door for
inspiration and continues to be an ambassador for Island food.

Publisher's note: While every care has been taken in compiling the recipes and text for this
book, neither the publisher nor any person involved in the preparation of this publication
accept any responsibility for errors or omissions, inadvertent or otherwise, nor for any
problems that may arise as a result of preparing these recipes.

Medina Publishing

Earl Mountbatten Hospice

NAMMET

A CELEBRATION OF ISLE OF WIGHT FOOD AND DRINK

IN AID OF EARL MOUNTBATTEN HOSPICE

EDITED BY CAROLINE GURNEY CHAMPION

CONTENTS

Foreword

Earl Mountbatten Hospice is the largest charity on the Isle of Wight, and for the last 35 years has provided care during the last years of life for thousands of dying and bereaved people. Most Island residents have a connection with our hospice and many will have been touched by its work through personal experience and direct involvement. When I speak to people across our Island community, they are quick to tell me their hospice story and their personal connection with it. These stories create a web of belonging which far exceeds any preconceptions or expectations. For these reasons, Earl Mountbatten Hospice sits at the heart of our unique community and plays a significant and daily role in both island living and island dying.

Linking Island local produce and the food that we eat to the work of Earl Mountbatten Hospice might appear to be a nebulous and unlikely task. However, food and the joy of eating remains as important a part of death and grief as it does of life and growth. After 30 years of working with the dying and the bereaved, I have come to realise that the things which are important to us whilst we are living become even more vital when we come to die. Pain and symptom management are widely thought to provide the cornerstone to good and effective end-of-life care. Although true, much of our work with those who are dying or grieving focuses on the psychological, social and spiritual aspects which make up the wholeness and essence of being human. It is not uncommon that families and friends cannot find the language to articulate their experiences. Favourite and good food often offers the opportunity for us to come together, and through sharing again common tastes and familiar ingredients and produce, we find the confidence to address difficult themes and issues. Sharing food can also help us put both ourselves and our damaged relationships with others back together again. We are therefore able to 'remember' and to reconnect with the best of each other in order to make life more bearable, manageable, as well as giving glimmers of hope for the future. As one bereaved relative recently told me:

> When we were at the Hospice, the chef cooked my husband's favourite meal. She managed to locate all of his favourite ingredients, and one of the biggest joys we had was to sit with him a couple of days before he died and share a meal together, the memory of which will stay with us all forever. We ate the same meal together following his funeral and I am sure that it will be something which we will share many more times in the future. It reminds us how much we loved him and how we were able to create good memories together at a time when our lives were falling apart. The experience provides us with a comforting memory and also gives us a hopeful glimpse into the future.

Sharing good food together with others is therefore essentially life-affirming. We are fortunate on our Island to have some of the finest local produce in the world. It is not unusual on our travels to see Isle of Wight produce increasingly sold and utilised both across the rest of the UK and in other countries.

We are very proud of our Island; we are very proud of our wonderful local producers; we are very proud of our Hospice. In this book, we share with you willingly and generously the best of who we are, in true Isle of Wight spirit. The fact that this book supports and affirms the work of Earl Mountbatten Hospice, our local Island charity, is a very special and added bonus.

Nigel Hartley
CEO Earl Mountbatten Hospice

Introduction

Nammet: a Celebration of Isle of Wight Food and Drink profiles remarkable Islanders who make fine produce. It showcases a selection of the best of food and drink with Isle of Wight provenance as well as some of the Island's beautiful countryside. Among the book's objectives are to raise awareness of Earl Mountbatten Hospice and its ever-expanding outreach services, and to raise funds for the Hospice from sales of Nammet.

Nigel Hartley writes that most of us Islanders have had personal connections with the Hospice. He frequently hears our hospice stories. He also reminds us that there is a real connection between the joy of good food – the theme of this book – and the Hospice and our local community.

When I first met him in 2016, he floated the idea of a recipe book to help mark the Hospice's 35th anniversary. He envisaged a sequel to *The Isle of Wight Country House Cookery*, published for the Hospice in 1993, a book which centred on iconic Isle of Wight houses and their occupants who supplied their favourite recipes, some with three-course menus.

Over supper we agreed on a new book. And so *Nammet* was born and it has evolved in unexpected ways. Island personalities – the producers and their featured food and drink – have become the celebrities and focus. They have passion and dedication for their work and artisanal skills, and they show exemplary entrepreneurship in creating sustainable ventures and great Isle of Wight produce.

The combination of profiles, recipes, photography and design demonstrate the talent and creativity of so many of our Island inhabitants – dedicated, innovative, often colourful and eccentric people. Dozens of them have willingly and generously given their time, skills, ideas and energy. They are photographers, writers, a designer, editor and proofreader, chefs, teachers, catering students, other helpers and the producers themselves. They also include local potters whose plates and dishes are featured with the food. *Nammet* is 'Made on the Isle of Wight' and its contents entirely produced and contributed by Islanders.

All of them appreciate and support the services the Hospice provides and have willingly become part of a collective effort. In the same spirit, the Hospice and many other worthwhile causes on the Isle of Wight benefit from local community efforts and energy. This book is a testament to and a result of their selfless service and collective drive.

The producers and contributors to *Nammet* include native Islanders ('caulkheads') who have always lived here; those who have visited and chosen to come and make their home here, and others who have returned to their Island roots later in life. There are also other special ingredients: landscapes, ever-changing seascapes, sunshine, a rich heritage, a burgeoning arts scene and, of course, delectable Island nammet. Such diversity has for centuries provided the essential essence of what makes the Isle of Wight such a special place.

Those who have participated in *Nammet* are acknowledged and thanked at the end of the book by editor Caroline Gurney-Champion. With deep family roots on the Island, she has brought diverse Islanders and ideas to the table. She helped frame and develop this book's concept, sought out contacts and acted as project director and coordinator.

As well as thanking the producers and all who have participated in Nammet we thank those who have bought a copy of the book. Please continue to support the Earl Mountbattan Hospice and the hospice movement, as well as Isle of Wight food and drink. Enjoy.

Peter Harrigan
Medina Publishing

Chapter One
The South-East

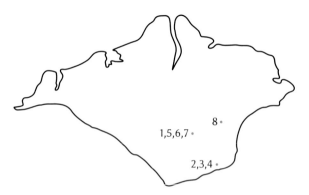

01. Angus Baird – Godshill Park Farm – Godshill
02. Chris Kidd – Ventnor Botanic Garden – Ventnor
03. Jim Wheeler – Fisherman – Ventnor
04. Maria Hakansson – Butter Vikings – Ventnor
05. Paul Metcalf – Natural Wight Mushrooms – Godshill
06. Stewart Pierce – Godshill Cherries – Godshill
07. Sue Browrigg – Brownrigg's Poultry – Godshill
08. Will Steward – Living Larder – Apse Heath

Reeth Bay

The South-East

The south-east of the Isle of Wight enjoys over 2,000 hours of sunshine every year. Benefiting from the micro climate along the south-east coast are three of the Island's towns: Sandown, Shanklin and Ventnor. The Undercliff between St Catherine's Point and Bonchurch is the largest area of landslip morphology in western Europe. Basking in the micro climate of the Undercliff, Ventnor became a popular resort during Queen Victoria's reign.

Today, there is a thriving arts scene and a popular fringe festival held every August. Inland, there are hamlets including Apse Heath and the mediaeval village of Godshill.

Angus Baird

Godshill Park Farm
Godshill

I'm the third generation of my family to farm sheep so I was brought up on a farm. My dad's parents originally came from Scotland before moving south to Hampshire. My dad and his brother moved to the Isle of Wight in 1968, buying a dairy farm on the outskirts of Ryde. Soon after I was born, my dad and uncle sold the farm and moved to a 1,300-acre rented farm in Shorwell.

I was always interested in farming. When I left school I did an apprenticeship on a local sheep and arable farm for two years before coming back to the family farm for a year. Then it was off to Sparsholt College in Hampshire for a year-long advanced sheep husbandry course, followed by a diploma in farm management.

I came back to work at home until 2002 when my dad and uncle retired. That's when I started on my own, renting various bits of land and concentrating on sheep as that's what the land suited.

Now I rent 500 acres of grassland in Godshill, most of which is in Defra-approved environmental schemes designed to improve water quality and limit soil erosion as well as improve conditions for farmland wildlife.

I now have a total of 1,500 ewes consisting of 250 March lambers lambing indoors, and 1,250 May lambers lambing outside. All are grass- and forage-fed, producing lambs to supply Farmer Jacks in Arreton. Any excess go off the Island for meat production. I hope to expand the farm in the future – subject to land availability, of course.

All our sheep have electronic identity tags so the meat can be traced back to our farm and people know where it has come from. I want our sheep to have high welfare standards – that's really important to me and I do a lot to make sure the flock is as healthy as possible. It's the way it should be.

You can buy our lamb at Farmer Jacks or taste it at the Essex Cottage restaurant in Godshill. Farmer Jacks make sure the lamb is hung for at least 10 days before sale so it's properly matured. One of my favourite dishes is slow-roasted lamb shoulder. Our lamb tastes delicious. I'm not sure if it's because we look after the animals' welfare or because of the high-quality chalk downland pasture they feed on – or maybe I'm biased!

Rack of Lamb

Godshill Park Farm
Godshill

For 4

    1 x 8-bone rack of lamb, fat removed
    Sea salt and freshly ground black pepper
    1 x 2-piece pack of lamb neck fillet (approx. 250g)
    Oil of Wight
    3 sprigs of fresh rosemary
    2 cloves of Isle of Wight garlic
    1 teaspoon Dijon mustard
    White wine vinegar
    300g Isle of Wight cherry tomatoes on the vine

Turn the oven on to 220°C / Gas Mark 7.

Put a large frying pan on a high heat.

Halve the rack of lamb, then season with salt and pepper and add to the frying pan with a lug of oil.

Drizzle oil straight into the pack of neck fillet and season. Turn the racks of lamb and then put the two neck fillets in the pan. Sear the ends of the meat and keep coming back to the pan, turning each piece so that they brown all over.

Pull the leaves off 3 sprigs of rosemary and put into a pestle and mortar with a good pinch of salt and pepper. Peel the garlic, add to the mortar, and pound really well. Turn the lamb over. Add Dijon mustard to the mortar with a good couple of lugs of oil and a swig of white wine vinegar. Mix well.

Make sure all sides of the lamb are seared then use tongs to transfer all of it to a roasting tray. Spoon the dressing from the pestle and mortar over the lamb and put the vines of cherry tomatoes on top. Move everything around until well coated in the dressing. Sprinkle with salt, then whack on the top shelf of the oven and set the timer for 14 minutes for pink to medium meat, slightly less for rare and more for well done. Turn the racks over halfway through.

Turn the lamb over. If the tomatoes are colouring too much, lean the meat on top of them.

When the 14 minutes are up, take your lamb out of the oven and leave to rest for a minute.

To Serve: cut the racks into individual chops and slice up the neck fillet. Pile on a platter. Move most of the cherry tomatoes to the platter on top of the lamb, mushing the rest into the cooking juices. Stir in a good lug of extra virgin olive oil, then drizzle over the platter and serve with gravy, mint sauce and seasonal vegetables of your choice.

Chris Kidd

Ventnor Botanic Garden
Ventnor

I joined Ventnor Botanic Garden as Head Gardener in 2000 and now I'm Curator. I originally trained at Kew and have worked at botanic gardens in Europe and Africa. Being Curator is my dream job and the opportunities don't come very often so I'm very lucky to work at one of the great gardens of Britain. Our subtropical and exotic plant collection is unrivalled – plants that would normally be found in protected glasshouses thrive and naturalise out of doors.

Take our lemon trees. It's unusual to find lemons grown out of doors in the UK. They like warmth and an acidic soil that is very hard – almost like concrete. The unique microclimate of the Undercliff at Ventnor makes it possible to grow these and other plants that would struggle elsewhere the UK.

Lemons are just one of the many edible plants we grow here. A lot of the food in our restaurant – such as salads, squashes and more exotic products like golden berries – is grown on site. Golden berries are thought to originate from Africa but they thrive here in our gardens.

The job of Curator is varied and a large part is generating money to keep the gardens open. I work with a large army of volunteers, up to 20 a day, who work hard to keep the gardens looking their best.

My favourite part of the garden changes every day but the Giant Waterlily has a special place in my heart. I have been involved in growing and breeding it here and at Kew. Within just a few months it develops from a pea-sized seed to a plant with lily pads nearly 3 metres in diameter which can even bear the weight of a child!

Each individual flower only opens twice. On the first night the flower is white to attract the scarab beetle which acts as pollinator, attracted by the white flower and strong pineapple-like scent. On the second night the flower opens again, but this time it is pink in colour. We are one of only a few gardens in the world which has been able to cultivate the Giant Waterlily.

Ventnor Martini

Ventnor Botanic Garden
Ventnor

>
> 15 parts Mermaid Gin
> 1 part dry Vermouth
> Twist of lemon zest

Shake over ice, serve in frozen cocktail glass.

Lemon Refresher

Ventnor Botanic Garden
Ventnor

This recipe is from 2nd Countess Mountbatten of Burma (daughter of Louis Mountbatten, 1st Earl Mountbatten of Burma).

An extract from her letter to the Hospice:

> 'I am pleased to send you a rather unusual but favourite recipe we all enjoyed, which you may like to include.
> I acquired it soon after marrying Lord Brabourne in 1946. Our farmer's wife used it especially as a refreshing drink to take out to the very hot, hard working people gathering in the harvest.
> My family later also used it and it even spread to some of the Royal Family! It is very refreshing.'

> 600g granulated sugar
> 3 tbsp Epsom salts
> 1 tbsp citric acid
> 1 dessert spoon tartaric acid
> 4 lemons
> 1 litre of boiling water

Put the sugar, Epsom salts, citric acid and tartaric acid in a bowl. Add the grated rind and juice of the lemons and pour the boiling water over.
Stir and leave to stand overnight. Strain and bottle. Dilute to taste.

Jim Wheeler

Fisherman
Ventnor

There's been a Wheeler fishing on the Isle of Wight ever since the 1400s, and Wheeler's Bay, on the Island's south coast, is named after my family. My father initially didn't continue the family fishing tradition, as it was almost impossible then to earn a living from it. Instead, he worked as a longshoreman on Ventnor beach, and latterly Steephill Cove, supervising the deckchair and canoe rentals. Then he took up fishing again, and my brother and I joined him as soon as we left school – against his advice, but there was no stopping us!

We go out fishing every day for crab and lobster, mackerel too sometimes, and use all the seafood we catch in our restaurant, The Crab Shed. The crab pasties and crab sandwiches are hugely popular – so much so that we now have to buy in crab from other local fishermen to meet customer demand, but they all come from the same water, just a little further along the coast! We added crab burgers to our menu last summer, which went down really well, and lobsters are cooked to order every day. My favourite dish, though, is our mackerel ciabatta, with griddled mackerel fillets, red onions and a lime mayonnaise. It's absolutely delicious.

We're lucky enough to live and work at Steephill Cove, a mile down the coast from Ventnor. It's a stunning spot, but it's incredibly exposed, and the most challenging thing about fishing these waters is getting the boats on and off the beach here. There's absolutely no shelter, and you're completely exposed to the south-west winds, with a groundswell to contend with and a very narrow entrance to land the boat in. But I can't say I've ever had any desire to leave the island. The only question really was ensuring we could earn a living here, and thankfully that seems to have worked out!

Wheeler's Crab

Jim Wheeler
Ventnor

It had to be a crab recipe.

I've always liked the combination of crab served with tomatoes but they do have to be sweet. Best to use Isle of Wight baby plum tomatoes or if out of season add a bit of sugar. The combination of the fresh crab with tomatoes, chilli, wine and buttery garlic crumbs is really good, and easy to make. One for a dinner party. You do have to love garlic though!
Crab shells make good containers for these bakes, or use large ovenproof ramekins.
Freezable. Reheat for 20 mins from frozen.

For 4
500g fresh crab – use a higher ratio of white meat for best results
350g fresh baby plum tomatoes chopped
Oil of Wight and a little butter for frying
2 onions finely chopped
50mls dry white wine
Pinch of dried hot chilli flakes
Breadcrumbs (2 or 3 thick slices)
15g butter
Small bunch of parsley
8–10 cloves of Isle of Wight garlic, very finely chopped
Salt and pepper

Heat the oven to 180°C / Gas Mark 4
Melt the butter in a small pan and briefly sizzle one clove of crushed garlic before adding enough breadcrumbs to top your bakes. Stir in a little of the parsley.
Fry the onions in butter and olive oil over a gentle heat until softened, then add all the chopped garlic, and cook for another minute or so ensuring the garlic neither burns nor remains raw. Turn up the heat and splash in the wine, tomatoes, chilli and salt and pepper. Cook this mixture for around 5 minutes until the tomatoes cook down a little then mix in the brown crab meat, you may need to add a pinch of sugar if the tomatoes lack sweetness.
Then add the fresh chopped parsley and fold in the flakes of white crab meat. You can add some more breadcrumbs to firm up the mixture if it's too wet. You want to eat this with a fork not a spoon!
Spoon into the shells or bowls and then top with your buttery breadcrumbs.

Maria Hakansson

Butter Vikings
Ventnor

We moved from Sweden to Ventnor is 2016 because the cream on the Isle of Wight is sensational!

I trained as an engineer in wood technology and manufacturing and I have also studied sustainable development. I've also worked for Ikea, as a politician for my local council in Sweden and even helped run a jazz club.

The other half of Butter Vikings is my partner, Patrik Johansson. Patrik's grandmother was a traditional butter-maker but he tried his hand at different careers before he followed in her footsteps. He has been a coffee grower, a fisherman and a salt-maker but butter-making is what we both love. Together, we're a very versatile pair!

Industrial butter can be made within seconds but ours is entirely different.

Traditional butter-making is an ancient craft and we have updated it with our scientific knowledge and creative research and development. We make different types of hand-crafted, artisan butter and they all begin when we culture the cream for three days to get a much more complex flavour. When you taste it, you can tell that our efforts are rewarded with a depth of flavour you just don't get from industrial butter.

Using cultured cream is something the French know about – in fact, it was the Vikings who taught the French to make Normandy butter all those centuries ago.

We are perfectionists and have read hundreds of scientific papers to give us the knowledge to produce the very best golden lumps of butter. We supply to some of the world's top restaurants, including the prestigious Noma in Copenhagen which is regularly voted the best restaurant in the world. We also supply several Michelin-starred restaurants throughout the UK.

Here in Ventnor, we are close to the green hills where our cows graze nearly all year round. It's important to us to be close to our farmers, but we're close enough to London if we need to attend meetings and bring our butter to discerning chefs.

Our philosophy is to use the best natural ingredients, combine them with taste and artisan craftsmanship in a truly sustainable business.

What? Only A Potato! OMG!

Butter Vikings
Ventnor

For 4
       1 cooked (boiled) organic King Edward or Maris Piper potato
       Butter Vikings Chanting Butter
       Chives, carrots and red onion
       Lobster or crayfish
       Poppy seeds or wild garlic seeds (dry roasted)
       Almond flakes
       Micro leaves of dill and mini watercress
       Small flowers or rosemary flowers
       Butter Vikings Virgin Butter
       Vinegar, sugar, salt and pepper
       4 candles
       4 spoons

Slowly boil 4 small potatoes until they are really soft – about 20 minutes.
Take and fill four spoons with semi-solid butter – preferably Butter Vikings Chanting Butter.
Stick some chives into the semi-solid butter and put in the fridge to chill until the butter is hard.
Peel the carrots. Confit small pieces of carrot. Simmer submerged in salted butter until the carrots are tender and moist. This should take about 20 minutes.
Drain the butter into a bowl and transfer the carrots to another bowl to cool at room temperature. Add a sprinkling of sugar.
Take some cubes of red onion and cut them into small pieces and lay them in a little vinegar, salt, black pepper and sugar. Leave for at least an hour at room temperature. (You can prepare this the day before if you want a more intense colour.)
Dry roast the poppy and wild garlic seeds for a few minutes. Roast the almond flakes in a heated pan in a little salted butter. (You could try crispy bacon or mandolined sweet chestnuts but you need something crunchy)
Take the spoons out of the fridge. Be creative and first put small bits of lobster or crayfish meat on the butter, then the carrots, micro leaves and flowers. If you have some Butter Vikings Virgin Butter then dot very small pieces on the spoons as well. Put the spoons back in the fridge.
Just before serving add the poppy or wild garlic seeds and also the almond flakes.
Take four beautiful small plates. Cut a little slice off the bottom of each potato and stand one on each plate.
Light four candles and place beside each person. Wait for a minute or two and then surprise the guest with the incoming butter spoon filled with delicacies. Everyone melts the butter in their spoon over each candle and then, when it has melted, they pour over the delicious organic potato.

Paul Metcalf

Natural Wight Mushrooms
Godshill

I have been growing mushrooms commercially for the past six years. I used to be a single-handed sailor. They say that when sailors have had enough they should pick up an anchor, put it over their shoulder and walk inland until someone asks: 'Where are you going with that pickaxe?' Then they should stop and build a mushroom farm.

The rather less romantic reason why I set up natural Wight Mushrooms is that I was looking for a new, niche food business with a technical side to it. Exotic gourmet mushrooms fit the bill.

It's a business that's constantly evolving. We started with a low-volume, wide variety, direct-to-consumer model. We combined selling at farmers' markets with the large food service operations to supply restaurants. Although that was great fun, ultimately it wasn't very profitable so we took a long, hard look at the figures and changed our approach. We dramatically increased our volume and now supply bulk wholesale to the mainland while a few, small local veg suppliers look after our loyal restaurant customers.

Although we don't supply direct to consumers any more, you can see some of our mushrooms in the Mushroom Fruiting Chamber at Ventnor Botanic Garden.

There have been lots of technical challenges along the way which I have relished. And with every increase in volume comes a different issue to solve. Theoretically, growing exotic mushrooms is easy. All you need is to control the temperature, humidity, light, light cycles and the amount of CO_2 in the air. But even then, there is a mushroom god – and he likes to have a laugh.

One of the best parts of the job is people's reactions when they see these mushrooms fresh – the scent and vibrant colours are amazing. They have even been supplied as flowers and subjects for drawing.

When cooked, they can go through many flavours from mild and 'mushroomy' to meaty and bacon-like, to crispy and nutty. My favourite is the White Elm Oyster. It's succulent, with a crisp, buttery flavour. Personally, I like them pan-fried on sourdough toast with a soft poached egg on top.

Mushrooms On Toasted Sourdough

Natural Wight Mushrooms
Godshill

For 2
 125g butter
 3 cloves of Isle of Wight garlic
 250g Natural Wight mushrooms (mixed)
 2 slices of Island Bakers' sourdough

In a large frying pan melt the butter over a medium heat.

Add the crushed garlic and mushrooms. Fry for about 3 minutes until soft.

Take off the heat.

Heat a griddle pan over a high heat and chargrill the bread until you have deep golden grill-mark lines.

Top each slice of toast with the mushrooms. Serve with a crack of black pepper.

Stuart Pierce

Godshill Cherries
Godshill

Our family moved to the Isle of Wight in 1996 when I managed a farm and helped with the building of Farmer Jacks Farm shop at Arreton. The aim was to make locally sourced produce more available to the public and support our local producers.

In 2007 I joined the partnership to run the Cherry Orchard at Godshill. It was extremely run down and needed a lot of improvements so there was a lot of work to do. We planted new trees and cleared areas to grow new varieties. We also built a structure to cover the trees when the fruit is ripe to keep the birds out and to make sure the cherries don't split in the rain.

Now we have 4,000 trees with many varieties from traditional red cherries to dark red, almost black and even white cherries. These are very popular and can outsell red cherries but they are very difficult to store to keep them in peak condition so catch them when you can!

The cherry season is very short – from June until the beginning of August. They are all picked by hand so those six weeks in the summer are a very busy time when 30 pickers come to help us with the harvest. For the rest of the year, there are just two of us working full time.

Cherries are classed as a superfood. They are high in antioxidants and packed with vitamins. Plus, they taste delicious, of course.

My favourite cherry is the Hertford. It has large, deep, dark purple fruit. It doesn't crop as well as some more common varieties but the flavour is superb.

In 2010 we acquired a new area of land at Adgestone which had housed an old, overgrown vineyard. It took us 6 months to clear and prepare the ground but now we have 6,000 apricot trees with six different varieties of international Cot apricots. The land is south facing, so it's an ideal location for these sun-loving trees.

Apricots are not often grown in the UK. They flower earlier than cherries – often in mid-March when there is still a danger of frost which could damage the blossoms.

We are currently experimenting with growing greengages and other stone fruits. Watch this space.

Apricot and Cherry Crumble

Godshill

For 6

> 500g sliced apricots (about 16 small apricots cut in half: make sure they aren't too ripe or the filling won't have any texture)
> 2 green apples, cut into chunks
> 450g whole cherries, which you'll need to pit and cut in half
> 100g sugar
> 115g light brown sugar (substitute granulated brown sugar if necessary)
> 255g Calbourne Mill plain flour
> 115g butter at room temperature
> ½ teaspoon fresh nutmeg (grated)
> ¼ teaspoon salt

Preheat the oven to 180°C / Gas Mark 4

Wash and cut each apricot in half, and remove the stones.

Pit the cherries and cut each in half.

Peel the apples and cut into medium sized chunks (you should get about 8–10 chunks per apple). Place all the fruit in the bottom of a baking dish (20 x 20cm).

Sprinkle the grated nutmeg and salt on top of the fruit.

Mix the flour and sugar together in a small bowl and add the butter.

Mash and mix everything together with a fork, until you have a crumbly mixture the texture of wet sand.

Cover your fruit with the crumbs and bake in the oven for about 40 minutes, until the top is golden and the edges are starting to caramelise.

Serve on its own, with vanilla ice cream or fresh whipped cream.

Sue Brownrigg

Brownrigg's Poultry
Godshill

My husband Paul and I have been farming here on the Island for over 27 years. I was born here and when we were married and got our own farm, as well as sheep we started rearing a small flock of Christmas Turkeys each year. As this proved increasingly popular, we looked around and realised no one was producing eggs on the Island or oven-ready birds – and Brownrigg's Poultry was born.

We now have over 6,000 laying hens at our traditional family farm in Godshill and produce 100 eating chickens a week. Our products are stocked across the Island, in all Southern Co-operatives, at the local farmer's markets and Briddlesford Farm Shop, and in many small independent food shops.

We wanted people to know where food comes from so they could identify with the source and feel proud of slowly helping small local farming economies thrive, so we opened our own shop in Godshill three years ago. Brownrigg's Farm Shop & Butchery is a real family affair, run by my son and his wife, and allows our customers to come and find our products seven days a week.

As well as our poultry, we stock our own meat, including grass-fed lamb, Ruby Red Devon beef, Isle of Wight Bacon Company pork, and vegetables grown in our own polytunnels. Our cows are a traditional British breed which have a much better flavour as they are suckle-reared and matured later before slaughter, and the meat is then hung for longer before sale.

We do all our butchery at the shop. We have a butcher on site on Thursdays, Fridays and Saturdays, for recommendations and cuts to order. Customers can also shop online and on our website. The shop is very diverse; as well as our own products we also stock a range of specialist foods such as organic, gluten free, dairy free, vegan and vegetarian products and a wide range of Isle of Wight produce.

We are always looking for ways to innovate – our latest foray is into the world of smoking. We've just bought a smoker and will be looking to produce smoked duck breasts. We also dry cure our own bacon and make our own sausages. So, we really are the one-stop shop to visit for the full complement of local Island produce.

Chicken Thighs Wrapped in Bacon

Brownrigg's Poultry
Godshill

For 4

8 Brownrigg's free-range chicken thighs (skinless and boneless)
8 rashers of Mottistone Farm dry-cured smoked streaky bacon
Fresh basil (a handful)
1 tablespoon Oil of Wight
2 leeks
200ml chicken stock
200g garden peas

Season the chicken with a little black pepper, put one basil leaf on top of chicken thigh, then wrap tightly with a rasher of bacon, tucked in to stop it unravelling.
Heat the oil in a large, shallow casserole dish or frying pan, brown the chicken thighs on all sides. Remove from pan.
Cut the leeks thickly on an angle. Add to pan and soften in the juices for 5 minutes.
Return the chicken thighs to the pan, pour in the chicken stock and simmer for 25 minutes or until the chicken is tender.
Tear up half a handful of basil and add to the sauce.
Finally, add the peas and simmer for a few more minutes until the peas are tender and bright.
Serve with new potatoes or crusty bread.

Will Steward

Living Larder
Apse Heath

My family has been farming at Apse Heath since 1922. But while I was growing up I was encouraged to get as far away from the Island as possible. I trained as a chartered engineer and stayed away for 10 years. Then I had a Eureka moment and realised what I had left behind. I had such a contented childhood, and loved the outdoor life. I couldn't resist any longer, so I came back and it felt right.

We have 20 acres in all and the Downs stretch out dramatically in front of us. Living Larder is a big market garden situated in a natural bowl protected from the cold northerly wind. Five of us work here full-time and the number grows year on year, which is quite incredible really. We are producing fresh produce all year round so we have to be clever about what we choose to grow. It helps that the Island boasts high levels of sunshine, long days and an extended growing season, plus a mild climate.

To begin with we focused on the more unusual items. We catered mainly for the Island's chefs, but we realized that we needed to offer the usual, too – but just better than everyone else. Roger Sergent at The Taverners in Godshill was instrumental in getting that side of things going for us, along with Ben Cooke at The Little Gloster in Gurnard, and Robert Thompson in Newport – all places we love to eat.

We grow lots of different things. Some of my favourites are our Romano peppers, heirloom aubergine and the various chicories, but I also love our heritage carrots, green beans and fresh peas. We sell direct to restaurants, and to the public through our online shop livinglarder. co.uk. We also have a veg box scheme, which is growing in popularity. We started it two years ago, initially just for family and friends, but we couldn't keep saying no to people and now we have many regulars.

The ethos behind what we do is a massive thing for us. The best thing about this job is seeing the look on people's faces when they taste how fresh our produce is. As of last year, we have entered into an official organic conversion, having practised organic techniques since our inception as Living Larder. All of our produce is picked by hand and everyone who works here is encouraged to treat it like their own personal garden.

It's important to take care of the land around us. We have lovely hedgerows and wide field margins to encourage bird and insect life, with a total of eight acres for wildlife habitat.

Beetroot Brownies

Living Larder
Apse Heath

For 12

> 250g beetroot – roasted with the skin on. You can also boil, but I think roasting gives a more intense flavour.
> 250g butter
> 250g Seaforth dark chocolate, (70% cocoa solids minimum), broken into pieces
> 3 large free-range eggs
> 200g dark brown sugar
> 100g Calbourne Mill plain flour (you can easily substitute this with rice flour for a gluten free version)
> 100g of ground almonds
> 1 tsp of baking powder

Preheat the oven to 180°C / Gas Mark 4. Grease and line a baking tin – I like a deep brownie so I use a 22cm square tin.

Melt the chocolate and butter in a heatproof bowl over a saucepan of barely simmering water – once melted leave to cool slightly.

Purée your cooked beetroot until smooth – you can also grate if you don't mind the mess, but grating will give a different texture (a bit more like carrot cake) and more beetrooty taste.

Combine the beetroot purée with the melted chocolate. (If you've used a food processor to make the beetroot purée just add the melted chocolate and butter to the food processor and blitz a few times.)

In a separate large bowl whisk the eggs and sugar until well combined before adding the chocolatey beetroot mix.

Fold in the dry ingredients using a large metal spoon – almonds first, then sift in the flour and baking powder. Be careful not to overmix as this can make the brownies hard.

Pour the mixture into the prepared tin and bake for 35–40 minutes: be careful not to overcook as they will dry out, and everyone loves a squidgy brownie.

For delicious flavour combinations you could try adding 100g of chopped walnuts or 100g of halved, destoned Godshill cherries added just before the dry ingredients.

Storm Brian – Castle Cove

Chapter Two

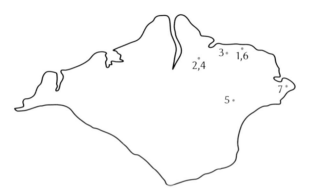

01. Fabian Game – Isle of Wight Distillery – Ryde
02. Helen Mcquire – The Borneo Pantry – Wootton
03. Matthew Noyce – Quarr Abbey – Binstead
04. Paul Griffin – Briddlesford Lodge Farm – Wootton
05. Rich Hodgeson – Isle of Wight Cheese Company – Alverstone
06. Ron Holland – Kemphill Farm- Ryde
07. Ruth Curtis – Captain Stan's – Bembridge

Ashey

The North-East

The north-east of the Isle of Wight faces the sheltered Solent and has four of the Island's six ferry terminals. The largest town is Ryde with its early 19th century, 703-metre pier, serving as a ferry dock and railway terminus. The area also includes the town of East Cowes on the Island's main river, the Medina; Bembridge, the largest village in the UK, and Wootton, site of the 1969 Isle of Wight Festival. Osborne House, Queen Victoria' much-loved summer residence is located on the outskirts of East Cowes and its extensive grounds sweep down to the shores of the Solent. The sheltered waters of the Solent are unique in Europe for complex tides and the long periods of stand at High and Low Waters.

Fabian Game

Isle of Wight Distillery
Ryde

The Isle of Wight Distillery holds the title of the first and only recorded distillery on the Isle of Wight, we're creating history and that's something we are really proud of. The Distillery was founded in 2015 and since then we've set out to create a premium range of products that reflect our laid back, Island way of life and capture that true Island spirit. Actually, our tagline is 'True Island Spirit' and with these values at heart we created each of our handcrafted spirits to taste like a sip of fresh sea air to try and evoke memories of a day at the seaside.

All our products are made using the highest quality fair trade and, where possible, local ingredients and we know the provenance of all our botanicals. Currently we produce four spirits: Wight Mermaids Gin, Rock Sea Vodka, HMS Victory Navy Strength Gin and Apple Pie Moonshine. Wight Mermaids Gin aims to capture the freshness of coastal air from hand-harvested local rock samphire and locally grown Boadicea hops, while Rock Sea Vodka is made using Isle of Wight spring water seasoned with a pinch of rock sea salt just before bottling.

A real coup for us is our HMS Victory Navy Strength Gin, which we have created in partnership with the National Museum of the Royal Navy. At 57% proof, inspired by HMS Victory, this is the first and only Navy strength gin to be sold and promoted by the Royal Navy and to carry their seal.

We are also distilling the first Island single malt whisky, brewed and distilled with Isle of Wight barley. Not many people realise that the base alcohol for whisky is beer. We have created a unique recipe using Island barley brewed locally at Goddard's Brewery before moving to the distillery. The new barley spirit is then left to mature in oak casks for at least three years, as governed by the Scottish Whisky Association.

For the first two years we were based at Rosemary Vineyard, but by the summer of 2017 increased demand meant we needed to expand. So the whole operation moved to Pondwell Hill, Ryde, where our passionate distillers work around the clock to produce our spirits in small batches according to our strict recipes.

We are currently stocked in Majestic stores and Southern Co-operatives along the south coast and across the Island, as well as in local independent food and farm shops. And we're also in many pubs, bars and restaurants across the country.

Isle of Wight Cocktails

Isle of Wight Distillery
Ryde

Salted Caramel Espresso Martini
50ml Rock Sea Vodka
25ml cold espresso coffee
25ml caramel syrup
25ml coffee liqueur

Shake and fine strain all ingredients into a Martini glass, garnish with 3 coffee beans.

The Bramble
50ml Wight Mermaids Gin
20ml lemon juice
20ml sugar syrup
25ml Rosemary Vineyard Blackberry Liqueur

Shake and strain the first three ingredients into a tumbler filled with crushed ice
and drizzle the blackberry liqueur on top. Garnish with fresh blackberries.

Marmalade Mermaid
50ml Wight Mermaids Gin
2 tsps English marmalade
15ml Cointreau
15ml fresh lemon juice

Shake and fine strain all ingredients into a Martini glass. Garnish with an orange twist.

Helen McGuire

The Borneo Pantry
Ryde

We have three generations of culinary wizardry in my family. So it's true to say cooking is inherent in our family gene. I grew up in Yorkshire, where my father and grandparents were bakers. It's no surprise that I studied hospitality management at Derby University, which included the basics of learning how to be a chef.

My love of cooking came to the fore when we lived in Borneo for five years. For our first Christmas in Brunei, in 38°C baking heat, I went shopping to buy chutney to have with our traditional Boxing Day lunch. But nothing was on offer, apart from Branston Pickle. So I made the chutney myself. It was such a big hit that friends started requesting for themselves.

Great feedback fed my desire to create a business, so I made bigger batches to cater for orders for both personal use and as gifts. The Borneo Pantry began in 2011 to keep up with growing demand from locals and the expat community. Soon I was showcasing my chutneys and relishes at craft fairs – the first one at Royal Brunei Yacht Club.

Showcasing at events is key for my products. When we moved to the Isle of Wight in late 2015, the business mushroomed. I showcased at events every weekend on the Island from the Garlic Festival and Chale Show to Barton Manor. My two boys, aged six and eight, like to help out at events wearing their Borneo Pantry T-shirts, while my husband helps assemble the gazebo. It's a real family business.

My range continues to grow too. I have a total of nine products– eight chutneys and relishes, and one pickled watermelon, which is unusual and interesting. My piccalilli is also very popular. But the range also covers caramelized onion marmalade, caramelized onion & cranberry marmalade, Christmas chutney, beetroot & apple chutney, spicy mango chutney, spicy sweetcorn relish, tomato red pepper & chilli chutney.

My aim is for Borneo Pantry to organically grow. I'm stocked in eight shops around the Island and for now everything is home-cooked in small batches of around 15 jars in my kitchen in Ryde. It would be great to develop a unit outside the house and employ somebody to work alongside me. Thirty jars of chutney weigh a tonne when you're carting them around events, so who needs the gym!

Stuffed Caramelised Onion and Cranberry Turkey Burgers

The Borneo Pantry
Ryde

On any given day of the week if you were to ring my doorbell you would be greeted by me wearing my pink onion goggles (and yes they do work, no more onion tears for me) and welding a large kitchen knife. Just ask the postman – it's a sight he has become accustomed to seeing. While the roots of the Borneo Pantry are tropical, the flavours produced are very much grounded in the UK. I am often asked, "What would go with this, how would you eat it, could you put it in a sandwich?" And yes, while chutneys are great with crackers and cheese, they are also very versatile within cooked recipes. Undoubtably the ying to chutney's yang is cheese and here I have paired my sweet yet sharp caramelised onion and cranberry marmalade with the Isle of Wight Cheese Company's Galleybagger.

For 8
- 1kg minced Brownrigg's turkey
- 65g of plain bread crumbs
- 1 jar of The Borneo Pantry's caramelised onion and cranberry marmalade
- 100g Isle of Wight galleybagger cheese, grated
- 1 Isle of Wight free-range egg
- 2 teaspoons mustard
- 2 teaspoons dried parsley
- 1 teaspoon salt; 1 teaspoon black pepper
- 1 teaspoon olive oil
- 8 burger buns
- More cheese and toppings for dressing the burgers as you see fit

In a large bowl mix together the minced turkey, breadcrumbs, egg, mustard, parsley, salt and pepper.

Divide into 8 equal portions. Form each portion into a tightly packed ball. Working with one ball at a time divide into 2 equal portions. Flatten them into a circle on a chopping board.

Place a heaped teaspoon of the caramelised onion and cranberry marmalade in the middle, top with the grated cheese and place the other patty on top.

Crimp the edges together to seal them. The marmalade and cheese will make a bump on top. Make sure none of the mamalade leaks out.

Repeat until all 8 burgers are ready. You can cook the stuffed burgers on the BBQ or under the grill, this will take about 5 minutes each side.

With the filling being precooked, they don't take long – but remember that it is poultry so you must make sure you cook them through. Serve on the buns with all the extra toppings . . . devour.

Matthew Noyce

Quarr Abbey
Binstead

I am the head gardener at Quarr Abbey, a Benedictine monastery. It's situated on the north coast of the Isle of Wight, nestled between Fishbourne and Binstead. Visible from far and wide, the bell tower reaches skyward calling the monks to prayer seven times a day. Monk architect Dom Paul Bellot designed the imposing buildings and construction took place between the years of 1908 and 1914 using skilled island tradesmen.

It is surrounded by fertile fields on which the Abbey grows crops and grazes livestock. A historic walled garden surrounds the most fertile ground. Early aerial photographs show a hugely productive walled garden and many livestock systems across the estate.

The monastery has a history of self-sufficiency. Along with my team, we have helped to restore that emphasis. Mindful of the sensitivity of Quarr, much thought has been given to what was enhanced and what produce is grown. I gained qualifications at Sparsholt College and my previous positions include head gardener at Lainston House, near Winchester, coastal ranger in Cornwall, countryside ranger in Hampshire and senior arboriculturist at Sir Harold Hillier Gardens.

We have created a growing plan featuring interesting and old heritage varieties. These provide noticeably flavoursome, if sometimes rather knobbly, produce. It has been rewarding to help secure a future for plants, which may otherwise be lost to more recent commercialisation in growing techniques.

Quarr Abbey was awarded the National Farmers' Union Conservation Award for good land management practices. We have taken a more labour-intensive approach to growing by choosing not to use potentially harmful chemicals. As custodians of the land, it is our responsibility to maintain and manage for future generations.

We have also founded a social enterprise project. It provides a number of charities, which have members with all abilities, an opportunity to grow produce in their own vegetable plots on Quarr Abbey land.

The Abbey's home-grown range has flourished over recent years. Now it provides an impressive array of produce that is used within the Abbey and teashop kitchens and is sold in the Quarr Abbey farm shop. It includes over 150 varieties of vegetables, herbs, fruits and plants, our 'orchard blend' apple juice and ciders, our award winning Quarr Abbey Ale, homemade jams and chutneys, eggs from our rescued hens in retirement, honey from our apiaries kept in our fields and orchards and pork from our own pig herd raised by the monks.

Oven Top Lamb Casserole with Winter Vegetables

Quarr Abbey
Binstead

At Quarr Abbey we are blessed with an abundant choice of organically grown vegetables and herbs from our monastery garden all year round. This hearty and healthy casserole does not take long to prepare. Use whatever vegetables are available. Stewing beef can be used instead of lamb.

For 8

2 tbsp Oil of Wight
500g Godshill Park lamb stewing meat (or beef)
250ml dry red wine. Dry cider also works well
2 Isle of Wight garlic cloves, peeled and minced or finely chopped
1 tbsp fresh thyme, chopped
Good pinch salt
level tsp ground black pepper
1 bay leaf
500ml good vegetable stock. Try making your own
2 medium sized onions, peeled and roughly diced
3 celery sticks chopped into chunks
150g parsnip, peeled and sliced. Use potatoes as an alternative, or 50/50
150g swede, peeled and cut into chunks
3 medium sized leeks
150g pearl barley
125ml sour cream
3 tbsp plain flour

Heat the oil in a large lidded saucepan and gently brown the lamb/beef on all sides.
Drain the fat and add the wine or cider. Add the garlic, thyme, salt and black pepper
and the bay leaf. Bring contents to the boil. Reduce the heat, put on lid and simmer for 20 minutes.
Add the onions, celery, parsnip or potato or 50/50, the swede and the leeks and pearl barley.
Bring contents to the boil then lower heat and simmer for a further 30 minutes or when the vegetables are cooked.
Taste if you need to add more seasoning.
Pour the sour cream into a small bowl and blend in the flour. Slowly add 125mls of the hot stew liquor into the bowl and blend mix well.
Remove the bay leaf from the saucepan. Stir the sour cream mix into the saucepan and keep stirring until thickened.

Cuthbert's Fruit Cobbler

Quarr Abbey
Binstead

This recipe is in honour of Abbot Cuthbert Johnson, a retired Abbot of Quarr Abbey who died in January 2017.

We are richly blessed with the bounty of our orchards and soft fruits from our monastery garden. Most fruits can be used in this recipe but you will need to vary the amount of sugar you use. Taste fruit mixture first before baking.

For 6

For the fruit
700g Quarr Abbey cooking apples – you can use sweeter apples but cut down the amount of sugar to about 4 tbsp
700g of blackberries or other berries
6 tbsp sugar
5 tbsp Calbourne Mill plain flour
1 tbsp melted butter

For the topping
150g Calbourne Mill plain flour
2 tsp of baking powder
60g unsalted butter
3 tbsp sugar
120ml Briddlesford full cream milk with a dash of lemon juice

Preheat oven to 190°C / Gas Mark 5
Peel, core and roughly chop the apples and mix in the blackberries, sugar, melted butter and flour. Put contents into a lightly oiled 20cm ovenproof dish.
Sift the remaining flour and baking powder together into a baking bowl.
Add the cooled melted butter and rub the mixture with your fingers until it looks like breadcrumbs. Stir in the remaining sugar and milk.
Drop spoonfuls of this mixture onto the fruit. You don't have to completely cover the top – you want a cobbled look.
Bake for 35 minutes or until the fruit is soft and the topping is risen and lightly browned.
Serve with plain yoghurt or pouring cream.

Misty Morning Ashey

Littletown

Paul Griffin

Briddlesford Lodge Farm
Wootton

Farming is most definitely a family affair for us. There are six partners: me, my wife Chris, Mum and Dad and my two sisters. Briddlesford Lodge Farm has been home to the Griffin family since 1923 when my great-grandfather Charles Griffin walked the original 12 Guernsey cows across the Downs to take up the tenancy at Briddlesford. Since then, the farm has been passed down through the generations and my Dad, Richard, bought the farm outright in the 1980s.

Our 150-strong, award-winning herd of pedigree Guernseys are all descended from those original 12 cows and are ranked among the best-performing herds in the world.

We don't homogenise our milk, so Briddlesford milk is very typically 'Guernsey'. We measure each cow's milk yield and keep detailed production records of protein and fat content so that we get the best out of each individual cow. That also means that we know exactly where the milk has come from.

I'm often asked why we chose to stick with this traditional breed when so many other farmers changed to higher-yielding Friesian or Holstein black-and-white cows. The first answer is that we're extremely proud of our Guernsey cows and the animals are much loved and cared for. But secondly, it is the taste. Guernsey cows produce richer and creamier milk of a more 'golden' colour – just how milk used to taste.

Milk is far too often taken for granted as a lesser ingredient when it can be the most important part of your coffee, tea, breakfast cereal or dairy dessert. I don't have a favourite recipe for our milk because I think it is perfect on its own. It's a wonderfully refreshing drink – and it's good for you, too.

In recent years it has been recognised that milk from Guernsey cows can be attributed to extra health benefits. It has 33% more vitamin D, 25% more vitamin A, 12% more protein and 15% more calcium than ordinary milk.

We're now using our Guernsey milk and cream to make cheese, butter and clotted cream and this year we are completing a major new development in the form of a modern milk processing building. This will enable us to break free from a conventional milk contract and process all our own milk at home on the farm.

Briddlesford Halloumi Skewers Served on Giant Couscous

Briddlesford Lodge Farm
Wootton

This dish really shows off the rich flavour of our Briddlesford halloumi and the skewers can incorporate vegetables and even fruit when in season such as locally grown broccoli, asparagus, and plums.

For 4

For the skewers
2 red peppers
1 red onion
2 yellow peppers
4 tomatoes
4 flat mushrooms
Mary Case's Honey Mustard Dressing
2 wheels of Briddlesford halloumi

For the giant couscous
1 red onion
200g giant couscous
400ml vegetable stock
Knob of butter/dash of white wine
White wine vinegar, tsp sugar
Salt and freshly ground black pepper

Put 4 long skewers in water to soak for a few minutes.
Cut all your chosen vegetables and fruit into nice big chunks – aim to give as much drama as possible to your dish! Then pan fry briefly to give a nice colour.
Thickly slice the halloumi and then gently push all the items onto the damp skewers. Alternate colours and flavours as appropriate and stand on a baking tray. Drizzle generously with honey mustard dressing.
Finely dice another red onion and sauté for 3 minutes in a pan, add a little butter and sugar and cook for a further minute to release the natural sugars.
Add a dash of white wine and white wine vinegar and cook for a further 2 minutes. Now add the couscous and stir thoroughly into the mix.
Add almost 400ml vegetable stock and stir continuously to soak up the giant couscous. Add more stock if necessary until couscous is cooked thoroughly.
This should take about 15 minutes. Meanwhile, pre-heat the oven and bake the skewers for 10 minutes. Tip the couscous onto a large serving dish, arrange the skewers on top and serve with a green salad. Wait for the applause!

Richard Hodgeson

The Isle of Wight Cheese Company
Alverstone

I started the cheese company in 2006 with my Mum, Julie. I was born in Newcastle but I grew up in West Wight. After studying in the north-east, I was working as a television editor but became a bit disillusioned so I began looking for a new challenge. I jumped on an idea that my Mum and one of her friends had about making cheese here on the Island, so after eight years away I came back to make cheese.

The milk that we use influences the flavour of our cheese. Our cheese business is situated at Queen Bower Dairy, near Sandown. We took on the dairy business in 2017 from the farmer Michael Reed after he retired. We use our own milk from our cows and also from our friends the Griffins, at Briddlesford. Flavour and freshness of the milk is needed when making cheese and I'm proud to be able to produce my own milk and buy from a local island farm too.

The three cheeses that the business has been built on are Isle of Wight Soft – this is close to Camembert; Gallybagger, which is an unpasteurised cheddar-style cheese; and Isle of Wight Blue, which when ripe is a spreadable soft blue cheese. In 2018, we added two new cheeses: Blue Slipper which is a softer surface ripened blue, and Borthwood Brie which is a milder, softer, white-rinded cheese.

Our Isle of Wight Blue won Best English Cheese at the World Cheese Awards. It's made with pasteurised milk and the natural rind of the cheese gives it bags of character and flavour. It really stands out on the cheeseboard.

My favourite part of the day is the moment when all the cheeses are made. You're looking at the transformation from what was milk about seven hours earlier. The aroma in the air from the acidifying cheeses is unlike anything that you've smelled before.

I think my proudest moment is seeing how impressed my Dad was with one of the very first batches. He sadly died unexpectedly very soon after I first started making cheese so he's never been able to see what has been built.

I'm really happy with the decision I made to return to the Island and the cheeses I make. No two days are the same when you're making cheese. The process may be similar day to day but your ingredients are always variable and the effect that has on how I make the cheese on a particular day is one of the challenges that I enjoy the most.

The Cheesemaker's Breakfast

The Isle of Wight Cheese Company
Alverstone

This is genuinely what I send myself off to the farm with most mornings

For 1
Tomato mix recipe (kept in fridge used all week)
Punnet of Isle of Wight baby plum tomatoes, cut into quarters
½ red onion (sliced thinly)
1 Isle of Wight garlic clove (crushed)
Handful of fresh basil, chopped
Splash of red wine vinegar

Add all the ingredients in a bowl and stir well. Transfer to a jam jar and keep in the fridge.

Seeded wholemeal loaf (Island Bakers)
Avacado (mashed)
Organic butter
2 slices of ripe Isle of Wight soft cheese
Salt and freshly ground black pepper

Take a slice of seeded wholemeal bread – toasted. Spread a generous amount of organic butter on top.
Then add some mashed avocado, two slices of ripe Isle of Wight soft cheese with 2 spoonfuls of the homemade tomato mix.
Lastly, add a twist of salt and pepper.

Ron Holland

Kemphill Farm
Ryde

I grew up on a farm in Oxfordshire, the youngest of five children. I left home to study agriculture and came to the Isle of Wight 45 years ago. For 27 years I was a dairy farmer, but I now farm beef with my son James.

I am what is known as a 'grazier'. I source high quality suckled calves aged 9–10 months old from other farmers and graze them on my land to produce beef.

Most farmers prefer to breed cattle but not fatten them, giving opportunities for those of us who wish to specialise. On the Island there are only three who finish cattle commercially. I need 200 cattle per year and the animal is with me for an average of 12–14 months. In order to get continuity of supply, I buy 15–20 suckled calves each month.

Most calves are born in the spring so farmers have difficulty providing meat throughout the year. I endeavour to produce a minimum of three fat animals each week. To do this, I feed grass or silage to appetite and only small amounts of grain when appropriate.

All my cattle spend seven months grazing the best grass I can produce at my farm near Havenstreet. The other five months they are in large, airy yards, eating farm-produced grass silage with added molasses, local wheat, minerals and vitamins.

Meat from older cows will be tough, so mine are not allowed to go over 30 months of age. My meat is hung for a minimum of three weeks, ensuring it is meltingly tender – I guarantee you won't get a bad steak.

I keep an audit trail so I can guarantee the provenance of all my cattle. This, combined with the continuity of supply, means I am one of only two cattle farmers on the Isle of Wight to earn the coveted Wight Marque.

Over the last six years, Kemphill Beef has become sought-after and it has become difficult to keep up with demand. Now I have an exclusive supply contract with Sam Shaw, the proprietor of the Fighting Cocks pub – so that's where you can eat the best beef on the Island!

Beef Wellington

Kemphill Farm
Ryde

For 4

1kg Kemphill beef fillet, trimmed
¼ bunch of thyme, finely chopped
Sea salt and freshly ground black pepper

Duxelles
55g butter
1 clove of Isle of Wight garlic
500g flat field mushrooms, finely chopped
A few drops of truffle oil
1 tbsp finely chopped parsley

Wellington
English mustard to taste
500g block of puff pastry
1 Isle of Wight free-range egg, lightly beaten, to seal the pastry
Melted butter, to glaze.
Preheat the oven to 18°C / Gas Mark 4.

Season the beef with the thyme, sea salt and pepper and set to rest for 30 minutes. Heat a pan and sear each side of the beef until golden brown. Allow to cool to room temperature.
For the duxelles, sauté the butter, garlic and mushrooms in a pan over a low heat until all the moisture evaporates. Add the truffle oil, parsley and season to taste. Remove from the heat and allow to cool to room temperature. Smear the beef with an even coating of English mustard.
Lightly dust a sheet of baking paper with flour. Roll the pastry so it is a little wider than the beef, and the beef can be completely rolled in pastry. Place the pastry so the longest half is facing you.
Spread the duxelle mixture evenly over the half of the pastry closest to you. Place the beef on top of the mushroom mix. Roll the beef up in the pastry, leaving a slight overlap of 3cm. Brush this with the beaten egg to seal. Trim the ends of the pastry so they are flush with the beef.
Cut a sheet of baking paper the size of the beef Wellington. Place the beef Wellington on the paper, lightly brush the top with melted butter and refridgerate for 30 minutes. Put the beef Wellington in the oven and cook for 25 minutes or until dark golden in colour.
Serve with steamed spinach or roast vegetables or whatever is in season.

Ruth Curtis

Captain Stan's
Bembridge

I spent 12 years living and working in Spain, where I first discovered my love of eating and cooking fish. Now one of my favourite dishes to make is a seafood paella, which I like to cook on the barbecue, using squid, prawns, monkfish or pollock and clams. But so long as the fish is fresh, just a simple fillet, wrapped in foil and baked in the oven for ten minutes, can be superb.

My husband Mike and I both once had 'proper jobs', but Mike had always fished as a hobby. When we came to the Isle of Wight on holiday, 14 years ago, we bought a fishing boat that a friend's son was selling, so that Mike could earn a living doing what he loves. We quickly realised two things: there was no fish market on the Island for him to sell his catch to (so he would have to take his fish over to Portsmouth to sell it wholesale). And secondly, there was nowhere for residents to buy locally caught fish. So we took on an old barge in the harbour and opened it as our first shop, before moving into Bembridge village four years later. It's such a friendly place, and we are so well supported by the local residents here.

We moved to the Island in 2003 from Cornwall, as it's got everything you need, and is an amazing place to bring up children. I love the open space, and relish walking down to the beach every day with our dog. I never get bored of seeing the same beautiful views every day!

There's quite a wealth of local fish, which varies over the course of the year. We regularly catch cod and Dover sole, bass, red and grey mullet, brill, and turbot, with a bit of squid from time to time, and lobster and crab all year round. We catch about 80% of our stock ourselves, and if we're short of anything in particular, we supplement it with fish from Cornwall.

I used to work in the Bembridge shop, and before that from our barge in Bembridge harbour, but now that it's so busy and we've opened a second fishmongers in Ryde, I'm much more in the background, making sure each shop has all the stock they need. I'm just the delivery girl really!

Grilled Plaice with Red Pepper, Chilli, Garlic and Oregano

Captain Stan's
Bembridge

For 4

4 whole plaice, approx. 400g each (trimmed and scored in both sides by your fishmonger)
1 small red pepper
½ mild red chilli deseeded and finely chopped
50ml olive oil
1 large Isle of Wight garlic clove finely chopped
½ teaspoon dried oregano
1 teaspoon sea salt
Freshly ground black pepper
Juice ¼ lemon

Roast the red pepper by placing it in a hot oven for 10 mins, cut in half, remove seeds, skin and chop the flesh very finely.

Put in a bowl with chilli, olive oil, garlic, oregano, salt, pepper and lemon juice to make a marinade.

Coat both sides of the fish with the marinade making sure that it is in the scores, and leave to marinate for about an hour.

Heat the grill until it's very hot.

Grill the fish for 5 minutes on a lined metal tray.

Firestone Copse

Chapter Three
Central

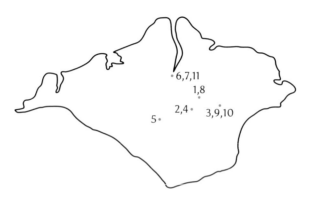

01. Ben Brown – A E Brown Farms ltd – Arreton
02. Carline Knox – Oil of Wight – Merston
03. Colin Boswell – The Garlic Farm – Newchurch
04. Fiona Pink – PINK'S – Merstone
05. Gillian Belben – Beekeeper – Chillerton
06. Gioia Minghella – Minghella Ice Cream – Newport
07. John Fahy – The Island Bakers – Newport
08. Paul Thomas – The Tomato Stall – Arreton
09. Krista Denton – Made by Krista – Newchurch
10. Tracey Sangster – Wight Crystal – Newport

Arreton Valley

Central

Located in the central area is the Isle of Wight's capital and its largest town, Newport which also hosts the annual Isle of Wight Festival. The River Medina runs south to north and is tidal up to Newport which was laid out, at the limit of the tides, as a new town in the 12th century. The inland area of Arreton Valley has the Island's most fertile farmland. The south-facing slopes of the chalk downland ridge that runs across the area provide ideal growing conditions for a wide variety of crops including garlic, sweetcorn and tomatoes and asparagus.

Ben Brown

A E Brown Farms
Arreton

I am the fourth generation of our family to farm in the Arreton Valley. Our company name is A E Brown (Farms) Ltd – A E Brown was my great grandfather. Over the years the farm has gone from being a mixed farm producing everything, to a mixed farm producing dairy beef and cereals, then just cereals, and now vegetables and cereals. Some of the vegetables we grow now are sweetcorn, asparagus, squash, winter brassicas, and smaller quantities of soft fruits, leeks, potatoes, salads and beans, but this changes every year.

The Arreton Valley is special. It has deep, fertile soils and a high light intensity, which both lend themselves to growing high quality crops. Throw in the Isle of Wight's climate, which is moderate by the sea (not too hot in the summer and not too cold in the winter) and you can start to understand why Isle of Wight produce is recognised across the country.

We are particularly well known for our asparagus. Asparagus was originally a maritime plant. In fact, it's still found growing wild in sand dunes up and down Britain and throughout Europe. It grows particularly well on the Island, because of our sandy soils, salty air and intense sun. The first spears start to appear in April. As we head into May, our fields become covered with spears of dark green asparagus all the way until the beginning of July, when the season ends.

Every stem must be handpicked. During the height of the season, we have to harvest the crop twice each day. On a sunny day the spears can grow up to 15cm. It's important to cut the asparagus before the flower heads open: the hotter the weather the sooner this happens and nobody wants a flowery spear of asparagus.

Bigger stalks are great for barbecuing or roasting with a drizzle of olive oil. The slenderest stems are delicious in a stir-fry, or just simply steamed and dressed with melted butter.

We have supplied asparagus for the Royal Wedding, and for the Queen's Jubilee, as well as a number of Michelin-starred restaurants. On the Island, we sell our produce in our own farm shop in Arreton, and in independent greengrocers, and farm shops and delis across the south coast of England.

British asparagus is one of the last seasonal vegetables with which imports cannot compete. The flavour produced by our climate is unique and appreciated by asparagus lovers everywhere – and we like to think the Isle of Wight's climate, in particular.

Asparagus Wrapped in Parma Ham

A E Brown Farms

Arreton

Nothing is better with fresh asparagus than butter, salt and pepper. The secret is first to buy fresh asparagus then to cook it perfectly. When selecting asparagus look for a dark green colour, the stems should be firm but flexible and the cut bases should be moist (this is where most of the dehydration takes place after cutting – as a rule of thumb, the bases will be wet for the first 24 hours after cutting, damp for the next 48 hours, and after this the base will be dry. (Five days after harvest the outer skin will separate from the inner flesh as the spear dries out). Cooking times vary from a flash in the pan for fried sprue (first pickings) to 20 minutes in the oven for a jumbo. When steaming asparagus, look for a change in the colour of the spears from a pastel green to a bright green – somewhere between 4 and 7 minutes depending on the thickness of your spears. Overcooked asparagus is tasteless, stringy and, most of all, disappointing no matter what the sauce or the wrapping. Perfectly cooked asparagus should support itself when held horizontally at the base and wobbled a little. It can be eaten raw so under cooking is better than over cooking.

For 4
    12 medium to thick spears of Farmer Jacks asparagus
    12 slices of Parma ham
    Olive Oil
    20g parmesan cheese (grated)
    1 lemon
    A handful of flat leaf parsley – chopped
    Black pepper

Wash the asparagus and peel the skin from the bottom 2cm of the spears.
Pre heat the oven to 180°C / Gas Mark 4.
Heat a griddle pan on a medium to high heat and brush the asparagus spears with olive oil. Griddle the asparagus for a minute on each side or until dark brown lines appear on the spears.
Remove the spears from the pan, pat dry and wrap in the Parma ham, place in an oven proof dish drizzle with olive oil, cover with tin foil and place in the oven for 10 minutes.
Remove the tin foil, grate over the parmesan cheese and return to the oven for 5 minutes.
Once the parmesan has melted place 3 spears on each plate, dress with lemon juice, olive oil, black pepper and chopped parsley.

Caroline Knox

Oil of Wight
Merstone

Oil of Wight was born from a family conversation about how we could add value to what we were already growing on our farm. We've been farming at Merstone since 1983 and always grew rapeseed and so oil looked like the obvious choice. We use a simple cold pressing technique which produces a lower yield, but highly flavoursome culinary oil, that is gently extracted from the seeds.

We've been producing Oil of Wight since 2009. We make about 5,000 litres a year. The oil is really popular with local chefs who order significant quantities and often list Oil of Wight as a locally sourced ingredient on their menus.

From the very beginning Oil of Wight has been well received, by retail outlets, chefs and consumers. My first trip around the Island, trying to secure shelf space, with a boot full of bottles was an uplifting experience. I had such a positive reception to the bottles and also discovered the wealth of outlets and potential the oil had across the Island.

We sell our oil to Island producers as a key ingredient in their products, such as the gorgeous bakery goods from Island Bakers and the range of condiments and dressings made by Wild Island. Currently our oil is also sold at most of the farm shops and butchers on the Island, the Southern Co-Operative, and many independent retailers – so I've certainly got my work cut out.

If you see the fields of rape across the West Wight in early summer, chances are you'll probably be dipping your bread into oil made from it the following year. We don't grow the rape ourselves anymore – our farm has diversified to only produce crops for bio-mass harvesting, but we still only use Isle of Wight rapeseed.

Making the oil is very straightforward. I do it all here in Merstone. I buy the seed at harvest time from IOW Grain, it's dried, cleaned and stored in a huge container. It's then fed into a press where it's pressed into oil, which is filtered and put in a bottle.

As well as being a healthy oil choice, our oil is so versatile. It's rich in omega 3,6 and 9, and is naturally high in vitamin E. It's ideal for cooking, with half the fat of olive oil and a high smoke point, while its smooth texture allows it to be dipped, drizzled and poured.I recently had the label rebranded so now, as well as buying a bottle of oil you have a postcard of the Island to remind you of the wonderful scenery we enjoy here.

Courgette Cake

Oil of Wight
Merstone

This recipe is a family favourite Courgette (or 'Dinosaur Scale') Cake. It really is VERY good!

> 250g courgettes
> 2 large Isle of Wight free-range eggs
> 125ml Oil of Wight
> 150g caster sugar
> 225g Calbourne self-raising flour
> ½ tsp bicarbonate of soda
> ½ tsp baking powder
> 2 x 21cm sandwich tins
>
> Filling
> 200g Green Barn goat's cheese
> 100g icing sugar (sieved)
> Juice and zest of one lime

Preheat the oven to 180°C / Gas Mark 4.
Grease 2 x 21cm sandwich tins.
Coarsely grate the courgettes.
Put Oil of Wight, eggs and sugar into a bowl and whisk until creamy.
Sieve in the flour, bicarb and baking powder and mix.
Stir in the grated courgettes.
Pour mix into tins and bake for 30 mins.
Turn out onto wire rack after allowing to cool for a few minutes.
Filling: Combine all ingredients. Fill cake when cool and refrigerate. Dust with icing sugar and ENJOY!

Colin Boswell

The Garlic Farm
Newchurch

Farming is in our blood, it is our way of life.

I was born on a small farm in north Kent before my family moved to the Isle of Wight for the warmer climate and to explore the greater agricultural potential the Island offered. My father was ambitious for himself and the family and he pioneered the growing of sweet corn within the UK, supplying the expanding supermarkets from the 1960's.

My wife Jenny and I joined my parents' farm in 1976 after a spell working in London in market research and advertising – nothing like farming! Over the next 20 years the farm grew from a modest 300 acres to a massive 1,500 acres, importing 2,500 tonnes of garlic a year to supply the major UK supermarkets with fresh garlic, extending to fresh peeled garlic and garlic puree. In 1999 we sold this portion of the business and returned to our roots as a family farming business with a specialism in garlic.

Ours is a true family business and all of our five children get actively involved throughout the year. Our eldest daughter Natasha is now managing director of The Garlic Farm and our younger son Hugo manages the self-catering holiday accommodation we have on site as well as the website and social media. Our daughter Josephine runs her own mobile street-food business, The Garlic Farm Field Kitchen which is a big hit at many festivals and events up and down the country.

The product lines have diversified over the years and we now have over 70 garlic products bearing The Garlic Farm brand, including the legendary garlic beer and ice cream to the more obvious garlic mayonnaise and garlic butter.

The farm itself has grown and developed into a popular tourist attraction that centres around our shop, restaurant and 70 hectares of farm park where we welcome over 200,000 visitors every year.

My love affair with the bulb still continues and I am currently involved in exciting new developments in garlic in Israel, France, South Africa, Ukraine and the USA as an international garlic consultant.

The Garlic Kicker

The Garlic Farm
Newchurch

Our latest garlic taster – the Garlic Farm Kicker – a traditional Ukrainian medicine.

No one can appreciate the immense satisfaction derived from fresh garlic and cured pork fat until they have tried it. The pork fat protects the mouth from the garlic heat and again in the stomach. Vodka combines with the crushed garlic in the stomach taking it directly into the bloodstream. After two or three hits there is an appreciable increase in pulse rate after about half an hour. Try it!

> Farm cured pork belly
> Peeled garlic cloves
> Rock Sea Vodka served from the deep freeze

Take a garlic clove, slice into 4 even slices and roll each slice in a 75mm slice of cured pork belly (lardo in Italian, salo in Ukrainian).
Grind black pepper and serve.
Best accompanied by deep frozen shots of Rock Sea Vodka.
Alternatively take 75mm slices of cured pork belly, grill for 2–3 minutes under a medium grill and serve hot, spread with diced or crushed fresh garlic.
Deep frozen vodka is the best accompaniment.

Fiona Pink

PINK'S
Merstone

My great-grandfather, Thomas Pink, was one of the original Victorian business magnates, turning his family's fine food import business, E&T PINK'S, into one of the biggest marmalade and jam manufacturers of the late 19th century. The company was sold after the First World War, but he retained PINK'S wharf on the Thames as a storage facility, and I remember spending time there as a child with my father, planting the seed in my mind to re-boot the family business.

Initially, I worked in publishing and then as a business consultant in London, but when I moved with my family to the Island the time was right to re-launch PINK'S – with a contemporary twist but with the same ethos as my great-grandfather: quality foods to enhance everyday meals. I wanted to make food that could be used straight out of the jar, or used to cook fabulous meals in minutes – store cupboard essentials for today. We now have eight types of pesto, chilli jellies, chutneys and peanut butters, which are all cooked by hand and completely vegetarian. The pestos are perfect with pasta, but also make a versatile addition to dinner party dishes like chicken or fish.

I've always loved cooking and experimenting in the kitchen with various recipe ideas (such as watercress and wasabi pesto or chocolate peanut butter). Our family favourite is the Empire Chutney: a star anise-infused tomato chutney which tastes fabulous with curry. I felt huge pride when our Smoked Tomato Pesto was awarded Product of the Month by Whole Foods in Kensington, for selling over 350 jars in a month – a store record!

My work experience prepared me for the financial side of the business – vital in food retail, where margins are so slim. But being an Island-based company, we are supported by the local community, farm shops and gift shops across the island.

We moved here from London because we wanted to raise the boys outside the confinements of a city childhood. The Island – and Islanders – have allowed my family's commercial tradition to be renewed, and we all love living in such a beautiful place.

Fresh Pasta with Pesto

PINK'S

Merstone

For 4

    1 Isle of Wight free-range egg
    ½ tsp salt
    140g Calbourne plain flour
    2 tbsp water (some of which could be Oil of Wight)
    Pink's Rocket and Lemon Pesto
    20g parmesan cheese

In a medium sized bowl, combine flour and salt. Make a well in the flour, add the slightly beaten egg and mix. The mixture should form a stiff dough. If needed stir in 1-2 tbsp of liquid – either water or a mixture of water and oil. On a lightly floured surface, knead the dough for about 3-4 minutes.

With a pasta machine or by hand, roll out the dough to your desired thickness. Use machine or knife to cut into strips of whatever width you prefer.

Bring a large pan of lightly salted water to the boil. Add the pasta and cook for 2–3 minutes. Fresh pasta cooks very quickly. It will float to the surface when fully cooked.

Drain in a colander, serve on a plate or bowl and spoon through Pink's Rocket and Lemon Pesto.

Add some slivers of parmesan.

Delicious.

View from Bleak Down

Gillian Belben

Beekeeper
Chillerton

I inherited my father's beehives in 2005 and have been keeping apiaries in Chillerton and Rookley ever since. My hives might only be a mile-and-a-half away from each other but the honey they produce tastes completely different. I like a mixed flora honey, where the bees have visited a wide variety of fruit trees, hedgerows and summer flowers. It's quite an artisanal process, and I'm happy to have honey that's been collected slowly and results in a varied, intense flavour. My honey also seems to help some people control the effects of their hay fever.

Nowadays you have to put a lot of effort into beekeeping to get a good yield of honey. One thing you can never do is procrastinate: when the bees need something doing, you have to do it immediately, otherwise you risk losing them. If you don't look after your bees, they can suffer with pests and diseases, or may not have enough food to survive the winter. As a beekeeper, I can never go on holiday during May and June, as that's the season for swarming and I need to be around to keep a close eye on the bees. It's a demanding occupation, but endlessly fascinating – and the only hobby that actually pays its way! Plus, it's really good for the environment because you're contributing to the bank of pollinators.

Beekeeping was historically a rural pursuit, but now some beekeepers in urban areas are doing as well as those keeping bees in the countryside. Urban gardens often have a high density of interesting plants which bees thrive on, whereas intensively farmed fields and poorly managed hedges and roadside verges can become a green desert for the bee. It's fantastic that urban beekeeping is such a success, but it's also a huge shame that, thanks to modern farming methods and the widespread use of pesticides, the rural environment is not as welcoming to bees as it once was.

There's a great tradition of beekeeping here on the Island, with techniques being passed down through generations, from beekeeper to beekeeper. There is a huge variety of geology on the Isle of Wight, and much of the countryside that we most love – natural woodland, hedgerows, wildflowers on downland, in meadows and along our country lanes – is needed to support healthy populations of pollinators.

Persian Marble Rhubarb

Beekeeper
Chillerton

This is a recipe to inspire you to try something other than rhubarb pies and crumbles

>500g rhubarb
>2 tablespoons sherry
>100g honey
>250ml of Briddlesford double cream
>macaroons

Wash rhubarb, cut into small chunks and cook over a low heat with sherry and honey, stirring.
Blend and pour the puree into a glass bowl.
Stir in the double cream to marble and not mix; and chill.
Serve with more whipped cream if you want, and eat with macaroons.

This is not strictly a recipe, more a delightful memory of J B Priestley making a meal up at Brook Hill House in the late 1940s.

>"Making stew. It is not often I am allowed to do this; and indeed my great
>stew-making time was during the darker hours of the war, when anything was
>about a happen. But I am always delighted to make stew. And it is unusually
>good stew … One of my children, without any prompting from me, once ate
>four large helpings of it. My stew is thick, nourishing and unusually tasty. It
>has meat in it, but almost any kind of meat will do. I add all vegetables that are
>in season and in the house. And when I am in the mood I toss in exquisite little
>dumplings. After hours of simmering and thickening and thinning, for I never
>rush the business and keep peering into the pan, tasting, muttering a spell or
>two, I add any red wine I can lay my hands on, and then, at the last moment,
>drop in a spoonful of honey. The stew is then ready. The very smell is princely.
>Here is a stew that has been seasoned with many onions, red wine and honey
>– and my delight."

From 'Delight' – J B Priestly

Gioia Mingella

Minghella Ice Cream
Newport

Minghella has grown from humble beginnings to one of the most famous award-winning brands of ice cream in the UK. My father Eddie started the business back in 1950 when ice cream was only ever eaten in one flavour – plain! A typical Italian, he began experimenting with espresso, strawberries, nuts and liqueurs to create wonderful new flavours. When my brother Anthony and I were small my father would make us ice cream 'cakes' for birthdays. Fabulous! Ice cream seemed to make everyone happy, then, and I think it still does now – so I firmly believe that making ice cream is one of the happiest jobs in the world.

I joined my father in the family business after a much-cherished teaching career. I helped him grow the business into a host of prestigious outlets, from the South Bank to Fortnum and Mason, earning a national reputation for excellence and increasing the menu of ice creams and sorbets from 25 to over 240. How proud we were.

From the very start of the business, there has been an emphasis on balancing nutrition with luxurious quality. We have only ever used milk from Isle of Wight cows, not just for carbon footprint purposes (although that is very important to us) but because in our view it makes sense that the less polluted the grass on which the animals graze, the better the milk will be and the better it will taste. All our ice cream recipes are based on the philosophy that unless you put the best things in, you can't expect to get the best out.

My parents enjoyed over 63 years of marriage, but sadly my mother, Gloria, passed away in March 2014 and dad took the decision to retire fully in the October of the same year. Since then, Minghella Ice Cream has been run by myself and my husband, Richard, ensuring continuity in producing delicious ice creams that delight our ever-growing fan base.

In the summer of 2017 we merged with the Isle of Wight Ice Cream Company and moved the business to their fabulous state-of-the-art premises in Newport. Now all Minghella Ice Cream is made there, still with the same standards, recipes, methods and ingredients, by a wonderful team of people who take enormous pride in their work. We are so delighted that Minghella Ice Cream is part of our beautiful Island's heritage.

Crêpes Suzette

Minghella Ice Cream
Newport

12 smallish pancakes (around 20cms in diameter) made with rich pancake batter

For 6
- 200g Calbourne Plain flour plus pinch of salt
- 4 Isle of Wight free-range eggs
- 500ml of Briddlesford full cream milk plus another 200ml
- 50g melted butter plus more to cook pancakes

For pancake batter: Sift the flour and salt into a bowl. Make a well in the centre and add the eggs and milk, beating slowly until you have a smooth batter. When you are ready to make the pancakes – add about 200mls more milk, and the melted butter. Make in the usual way using a pan roughly 21cm in diameter When bubbles appear on the surface, and the bottom glides smoothly away from the pan, flip the pancake over and repeat. Stack the pancakes on a plate while you cook them all

Filling
150g unsalted butter, at room temperature
150g caster sugar
6 tablespoons Cointreau

1 large lemon (juice and rind)
2 large oranges (juice and rind)

Cream together the butter and sugar until light and fluffy. Slowly beat in the citrus juices, rind and Cointreau. Transfer to a bowl that will fit over a pan of hot water and whisk rapidly. Then place the bowl over a pan of cold water and whisk again until smooth and well blended. Spread half the filling across the pancakes, one at a time. Fold each one in half and then in half again, so that the filling is enclosed. Layer up the pancakes in a shallow, buttered ovenproof dish, and then dot with the reserved filling. Cover with foil and heat through in a hot oven –190°C / Gas Mark 6 for about half an hour.

To serve
3 tablespoons Cognac
6 twists of orange
6 scoops of your preferred Minghella Ice Cream.

Our famous Vanilla Bean is always a good choice or Salted Caramel or how about Celebration Orange and Grand Marnier – on the basis that you can never have too much of a good thing? Remove the dish from the oven and keep it warm while you flame the Cognac. Warm it slightly in a small pan and ignite (carefully!). Pour it flaming over the crepes and serve at once, decorated with a twist of orange and a scoop of your chosen ice cream on the side. Enjoy!

Ploughing Match

John Fahy

The Island Bakers
Newport

I run my artisanal bakery business, The Island Bakers, with my wife Helen. We're known for our wild yeast sourdough breads, and other baked goods, particularly our doughnuts.

We met in the kitchens at Buckingham Palace in December 2003. Helen joined our team of chefs, who were cooking for Her Majesty The Queen and the Royal family.

I once did a stage at three Michelin-starred Californian restaurant The French Laundry. After that I got a job as a chef at Michel Roux's The Waterside Inn, in Bray, Berkshire, where I worked for over a year.

My obsession with bread began at Gordon Ramsay's Tante Marie cookery school. Helen was already teaching there when I joined her. The more I learned, the more I got into bread – and then you couldn't stop me. I was making more bread at home than I could possibly eat. It was soon after that, in 2010, that The Island Bakers was born.

Our bread has a three-day production process for each loaf, including an 18-hour prove. For the first year we rented the kitchen at Bembridge Bakery during the night. But demand for our bread and doughnuts quickly grew, and so did our need for more space to bake.

We got a grant from Natural Enterprise, which enabled us to grow our business. So we moved to much larger premises in 2012 and we now supply top restaurants on the Island plus numerous delis and shops, and we continue to sell at the weekly farmers' markets in Ryde.

We opened our first café in 2014, as demand continued to grow. It's an ideal spot, near Farmhouse Fayre, at 89 St James Street, Newport. There we sell our bread, cakes and other delights, such as frangipane and cherry tart, Marmite pinwheels (think Marmite Danish pastry), roasted garlic and cheese scones, and Gallybagger (a local cheese) and potato focaccia, as well as selling coffee made using beans from local roaster Jasper's and Briddlesford Lodge Farm Milk.

Brioche

The Island Bakers

Newport

Makes 4 loaves
> 1kg strong white flour
> 100ml water
> 490g egg (approx 8 eggs)
> 20g salt
> 130g caster sugar
> 60g fresh yeast
> 500g salted butter
> Oil for proving bowl
> Butter for greasing tins
> Egg yolk for glazing

Ensure all the ingredients are room temperature.

In a free-standing mixer e.g. Kitchen Aid, mix together all the ingredients except for the butter, on the lowest speed using the dough hook, until combined.

Increase the speed slightly to moderate, and mix for 8 minutes.

Scrape down the mixture from the sides of the mixing bowl, then add the butter and continue to mix for another 8 minutes at the same speed.

Place the dough into a lightly oiled bowl or container and cover. Leave to prove at room temperature, until doubled in size, approximately 2 hours.

Tip out onto your work surface and divide into 4 equal portions.

Divide each of the 4 portions of dough into 6, and shape into 6 small balls. Repeat with the remaining 3 portions of dough. Place 6 balls, seam side down, into each of the 4 buttered 500g loaf tins.

Brush with egg yolk and place in the fridge overnight.

Remove from the fridge and allow to finish proving at room temperature.

Pre-heat the oven to 180°C.

Brush with egg yolk and spray with water, and bake for approximately 35 mins.

Paul Thomas

The Tomato Stall
Arreton

The Tomato Stall was founded in 2007 by myself and Jeff McDonald to showcase the amazing tomatoes we grow here on the Island. The business began taking freshly-picked Isle of Wight tomatoes to a handful of farmers' markets in London. We now supply farm shops, delis, retailers and restaurants throughout the UK, as well as a wide range of Isle of Wight businesses and our online shop.

Tomatoes have been grown here for over 30 years. We are based on Wight Salads nursery in the Arreton Valley. It's home to around 60 acres of glasshouse and a myriad of sustainable technologies.

The Isle of Wight benefits from more sunshine hours than most of the UK. It also benefits from the reflection from the surrounding water, which makes it a great place to grow.

We've come from humble beginnings. From just a small building, a couple of vans and a handful of employees, The Tomato Stall now operates across three premises, with a fleet of vans and more than 30 employees.

The Arreton nursery grows around 30 tomato varieties commercially. It trials up to 200 seed types annually in search of the best flavours. Varieties are carefully selected for their exceptional flavour, and every tomato is allowed to fully ripen on the vine ensuring the best possible taste. In 2014, Isle of Wight tomatoes became the only fresh tomatoes to have ever been given Great Taste Awards.

We operate a wide range of sustainable farming practices. It reduces waste, cost and the environmental impact of the business, and includes a completely biodegradable growing system and extensive rainwater harvesting. 2016 saw the opening of two brand-new energy centres which generate 22MW of electricity for Island homes while providing CO_2 and heat for the tomato-growing operation.

We also produce a range of artisanal products. Included in the range are pure tomato juices, sauces, condiments and slow-roasted tomatoes using 100% vine-ripened Isle of Wight tomatoes. We create all the recipes in-house, and introduce new items to the range every year to keep things interesting.

Tomato, Mozzarella and Basil Puff Pastry Tart

The Tomato Stall
Arreton

For 4

Ingredients
500g mixed speciality Isle of Wight tomatoes
1 x 320–350g sheet ready-rolled all-butter puff pastry
1 medium egg, beaten
25g finely grated parmesan cheese, vegetarian if preferred
1 buffalo mozzarella cheese, drained then torn into small pieces
2 tbsp olive oil
1 garlic clove, crushed
A handful small, fresh basil leaves
Sea salt flakes and freshly ground black pepper

Preheat the oven to 220°C / Gas Mark 7.

Line a large baking sheet with non-stick baking paper.

Thinly slice the tomatoes. Lay them flat on kitchen paper or a clean tea towel, sprinkle with salt and pepper and leave to drain.

Unroll the pastry onto the baking paper and brush all over with the beaten egg. Fold over 1cm of each edge to form a rim and pinch at the corners to seal. Prick the base here and there with a fork then sprinkle with the Parmesan cheese. Bake in the oven for 12–15 minutes until puffed up and golden brown.

Remove the tart base from the oven and sprinkle the base with half of the mozzarella cheese. Overlap the tomatoe slices on top. Mix the olive oil with the garlic, drizzle it over the tomatoes and then scatter the remaining mozzarella cheese on top.

Return the tart to the oven and bake for 5–7 minutes until the mozzarella has just melted and the tomatoes have heated through. Remove from the oven, scatter the basil leaves over and serve immediately.

Krista Denton

Made By Krista
Newchurch

The health & fitness industry has been my passion for over 20 years. Even from an early age, I showed real curiosity and interest in nutrition. I recall fond childhood memories in my family kitchen, watching intently as my mother and grandmother prepared funny looking raw fruit and vegetable juices.

My fascination with human sciences just kept growing. I qualified in Anatomy, Physiology and Cosmetic Science, as well as Beauty Therapy.

After spending ten years in London managing countless therapy centres across London I returned to the beautiful Isle of Wight. My husband is from the Island and some of our family are here too. We thought that it would be a wonderful place to bring up our son, and it has been.

My business started as a healthy hobby. I began to experiment with my own cold pressed raw juices and smoothies, developing and refining the concept further. With no additives or preservatives, the unpasteurised juices are enzyme-rich with the maximum amount of vital vitamins and minerals.

A thriving business emerged. After a frenzy of interest ensued from posting photos of my own juices and smoothies on social media, my cold pressed raw juice company

'Made by Krista' was founded in 2012. I love helping people achieve their optimum health aspirations by adding nutritious juices and a detox programme to their frenetic schedule.

The Island suits the cottage industry I run from my home. Because of where I am and what I do I am able to be there all the time for my son, family and friends.

My aim is to help others live a long healthy life. A daily raw juice incorporated into a healthy lifestyle has a profound impact on mind, body and soul – you can lose weight, boost energy, balance mood, promote good quality sleep – the list in endless. Healthy on the inside equates to external appearance too. Radiant skin, bright eyes, lustrous hair – even stronger nails; so you glow from inside out.

Three Juices

Made by Krista
Newchurch

Green Juice
1 x apples
½ cucumber
4 sticks celery
Kale (handful)
Spinach (handful)
2 sprigs mint

Red Juice
4 large carrots
1 raw beetroot
2 oranges
2cm fresh ginger

Yellow Juice
½ pineapple
2 grapefruit
2cm ginger

Blend ingredients for each juice in a nutribullet or equivalent. Pour into a glass and enjoy.

Tracy Sangster

Wight Crystal
Newport

We've been producing bottled water from a local water source in Knighton since 1989. The natural spring water was first tapped into in the 1800s and lies at the foot of chalk downland at the very heart of the Island.

I felt passionate about re-energising the business. After joining Osel, the parent company in 2015, I wanted to push the concept forward to ensure that both the community and local businesses understood what we do – and who we are, as charity plays a key role in how we operate.

We're not just about supplying water. When someone buys Wight Crystal water they are also supporting The Way Forward Programme. Profits from Wight Crystal go towards clients personal development- with a 24/7 support service for those living with mental health issues and disabilities. We also employ people at Wight Crystal that wouldn't otherwise find employment easily, helping people back into the workplace. They learn skills that encourage confidence and building a future within the workplace.

It's a growing market for us. Events are a key way of raising awareness and generating income such as Cowes Week, Jack up the 80s or the Garlic Festival. We want to make the public aware of the local community work that we do each and every day of the year. We now have over 700 water coolers supplying over 500 companies and homes on the Isle of Wight.

We are constantly revising our product range, so we can identify development opportunities with in-house produced flavours such as Ginger Beer and Traditional Lemonade.

We're constantly proactively raising standards. We have gained Customer service excellence, five star food hygiene rating and the Isle of Wight Chamber's Quality in Business accreditation. We're always looking for local support – it means a lot to us. Today, we provide support services to over 100 Island people with a disability.

Our long-term aim is simple: increase capacity to produce more profits which will create even more opportunity for The Way Forward Programme. We're very proud that money from every bottle of water sold stays on the Island. Every day at Osel is different. Co-ordinating both Wight Cyrstal and The Way Forward Programme keeps us busy in the knowledge that we are working towards a worthwhile final goal doing something we all immensely enjoy.

Vegetable Tempura with Soy and Sherry Dipping Sauce

Wight Crystal
Newport

Using sparkling water in your tempura batter makes a light and fluffy mixture, great for zinging up any vegetable or meat combo, especially if it is Wight Crystal sparkling water. There may even be some left over to make a lovely sparkling drink to accompany the dish.

For 6

100g (approx.) each of a firm mix of vegetables, cut into bite size pieces, such as aubergine, broccoli, courgette, mushrooms, red pepper, sweet potatoes
Tempura batter – mix this just as you are about to cook.
85g Calbourne Mill plain flour (sifted)
1 tbsp cornflour
½ tsp fine sea salt
200ml ice-cold sparkling water
A few ice cubes
Oil of Wight

For the sauce
3 tbsp soy sauce
3 tbsp dry sherry
3 tbsp sugar
Lemon (zest only)

Heat oven to 150°C / Gas Mark 2.
Mix together the sauce ingredients in a small bowl. Make the batter.
Put the sifted flour, cornflour and salt into a large mixing bowl. Whisk in the ice-cold sparkling water along with a few ice cubes using a whisk, but don't over beat. It doesn't matter about a few lumps. Use immediately.
Cover a baking tray with sheets of kitchen paper. Start to heat a deep-fat frying pan or large wok a third full of oil and have the frying basket, or slotted spoon to hand.
When the oil reaches 190°C dip some of the prepared veg briefly into the batter, shake off any excess, then lower straight into the hot oil. Don't crowd the frying basket. Fry for about 2 mins until light golden and crisp, then drain on kitchen paper.
Repeat with the remaining vegetables in batches, dipping into the batter just before you fry them and remember to let the oil heat back up to temperature between each batch. Keep the tempura warm in the oven, leaving the door slightly ajar so that they stay crisp. They are best served immediately on a warm plate with the sauce alongside for dipping.

Chapter Four
West

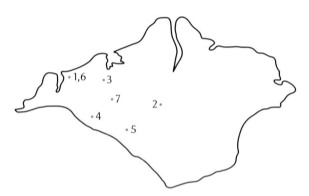

01. Abraham Seaforth – Ocean Creed – Yarmouth
02. Amy Lloyd – Splendid Brittle – Gatcombe
03. Chris Coleman – Island Brewery – Shalfleet
04. Jackie Carder – Mottistone Farm – Hulverstone
05. Mary Case – Beekeeper – Limerstone
06. Michelle Stevens – Green Barn – Bouldnor
07. Neal Smith – Calbourne Water Mill – Calbourne

Shalfleet

West

West Wight is predominantly rural, with dramatic coastlines dominated by the chalk downland ridge running across the whole Island. From Cowes, the indented coastline runs past the port town of Yarmouth to the Island's most westerly point. The dramatic south-western coast looks onto the English Channel and is known as the Back of the Wight. This area is dominated by the western half of the Island's chalk ridge which includes Tennyson Down and ends at the Needles, with its lighthouse and iconic sea stacks. The area is one of the most important areas in Europe for dinosaur fossils. The eroding cliffs often reveal previously hidden remains, particularly along the Back of the Wight. Dinosaur bones and fossilised footprints can be seen in the rocks exposed around the Island's beaches, especially at Compton Bay.

Abraham Seaforth

Ocean Creed
Yarmouth

I've always loved chocolate. It was something to share with family and friends. Like most of us, I think, it was an accumulation of shared experiences rather than a culinary epiphany, which I rediscovered when I was looking for a product that could promote emission free shipping of exotic raw ingredients by sailboat. Ocean Creed's story is that of the voyage of cocoa beans from bean to bar.

I discovered bean-to-bar chocolate when I started asking three simple questions – where is our food from, how did it get here, who makes it? Cocoa is an exotic ingredient that only grows in the tropics and is mainly shipped by sea in container ships. I met up with Fairtransport Shipping, which uses sailboats to ship cargo transatlantic, and I decided to create a product that draws attention to shipping practices of exotic ingredients and how it influences our environment.

Starting a brand that creates awareness of our environment needs more work, as every aspect needs to be considered. Ocean Creed uses an inner packaging called Natureflex, which is made from wood pulp sourced from sustainable plantations. It is compostable and biodegradable to 100% organic material within six weeks. Shipping cargo by sail is currently far more expensive, but a step in the right direction as it uses renewable resources for shipping.

I'm not from the Island, but I love living island-style. I love the sea and wanted to live near the sea. What better place to live than on an island, surrounded by sea and exposed to the elements. You feel alive here. We settled on Yarmouth, a beautiful, ancient village with the most magnificent wooden pier where the first few cocoa bean shipments were delivered by the Tres Hombres: solely reliant on wind and ocean currents as she has no engine on-board, and her visit was a highlight in the town.

The Island has other more obvious attractions, of course. I love to sail. I did my Coastal Skipper certificate in the Solent, and Yarmouth Sailing Club is brilliant for scow dinghy sailing up the Yar River. I particularly love Ventnor Botanic Garden and Steephill Cove – it's always sunny there when the rest of the country is under a thick blanket of cloud. Another perfect day here is a picnic on one of the Island's stunning sandy beaches, such as Compton Bay. It's hard to beat.

Banana Bread with Chocolate, Cocoa Nibs, Nutmeg and Rum

Ocean Creed
Yarmouth

This spicy, dense, moist quick-bread is strongly rooted in the Spice Isle, Grenada. The island you smell before you spot, approaching by sea on a tack. This loaf contains no added fat and is a firm favourite in our household as a snack or a desert. Demerara sugar contains more molasses than regular brown sugar and gives this bread a lovely hint of caramel.

200g Calbourne Mill plain all-purpose flour
1½ tsp baking powder
½ tsp baking soda
½ tsp salt
½ tsp cinnamon
½ tsp freshly ground nutmeg
1 egg beaten – Isle of Wight free-range
150g demerara sugar or brown sugar
50ml dark rum
3 mashed ripe bananas
1 tsp freshly grated ginger
1 tsp pure vanilla extract or I vanilla pod
40g finely chopped seaforth dark chocolate 70%
30g chopped pecans (optional)
30g cocoa nibs (optional)

Preheat the oven to 180°C / Gas Mark 4. Grease and flour a 2 litre loaf tin (23cm x 13cm).
Combine dry ingredients and dry spices in a large bowl or bag.
In a large bowl, combine the egg, sugar, rum, mashed bananas, fresh ginger and vanilla.
Pour dry ingredients into wet and combine with quick, light strokes. Do not overmix.
Gently stir in chocolate and nuts (if using).
Scrape the mixture into the prepared tin. Top with some cocoa nibs (if using). Bake in prepared oven for 50–60mins or until a wooden skewer inserted in the centre of the loaf comes out clean.
Let the loaf stand in the tin for at least 10 mins before turning out on a rack to cool.

Amy Lloyd

Splendid Brittle
Gatcombe

I was lucky enough to grow up on the Isle of Wight. In my childhood I was immersed in farm life in Shorwell. My parents farmed mainly arable, cattle and sheep, and also ran a fruit farm across from the main farm. I have wonderful memories of helping out by picking and packing the fruit: I guess from that early age my parents instilled in me the strong work ethic.

My biggest passion from an early age was food. I loved watching and helping my Mum and grandmother cook. Weekends were filled with baking sweet treats at home and entering local village shows with my creations. From the age of eight, I felt that my destiny was in catering (not farming!) in some shape or form – I actually preferred reading cookbooks to fiction! The gastronomic capital city of London was in my sights.

After studying catering and hospitality at the Isle of Wight college and completing my qualifications, I landed a job in a top restaurant, The Greenhouse in Mayfair. Gary Rhodes headed up the kitchen. It was tough. The hours were very long and intense. I had no social life for a while, but despite this I was totally committed. I specialised in the pastry section (desserts) and worked my way through the ranks in kitchens around the capital, learning and perfecting my skills along the way. I had the chance to cook for many famous people too, as well as renowned food critics, whom we chefs always spotted from a distance even though they thought they were inconspicuous!

A few years ago I decided to set up my own business. I had returned to the Island after I had my son in 2007 and had been working for the Garlic Farm as their pastry chef for nearly five years. Family and friends kept requesting cakes for various celebrations and so, with their encouragement, I set up Splendid Cake in 2013. It's a dream come true to be doing something that I love.

I was lucky enough to secure my own unit just outside of Newport in January 2016 and was able to build a kitchen for my requirements. Recently I have revisited an idea from a product that I used to produce for cake decorations – nut brittle.

I rebranded my products recently and I now supply them to various farm shops and select cafés around the Island under the name Splendid Brittle.

My business has now evolved into solely producing lovely nut brittle, as opposed to focusing mainly on cakes. I am currently developing new flavours and plan to sell directly online and make special bespoke gifts by post. Splendid ones!

Chocolate Fudge Cake

Splendid Brittle
Gatcombe

This chocolate fudge cake combines a voluptuous chocolate fudge sauce, which is incorporated into the cake mix, making it a devilishly moist and moreish treat.

For the sauce
50g 70% dark Seaforth chocolate, chopped
30g cocoa powder
Pinch of salt
150g golden syrup
40g caster sugar
100ml warm Briddlesford milk (if you are feeling extra indulgent then you can use double cream or a combination of both)

For the cake
150g salted butter
3 medium Isle of Wight free-range eggs
120mls of Briddlesford whole milk
70g dark cocoa powder

300g golden caster sugar
25ml Oil of Wight
1 tsp vanilla extra
190g Calbourne s/r flour

Butter icing
250g unsalted butter
250g sieved icing sugar
1 tbsp vanilla essence

Preheat the oven to 160°C / Gas Mark 3. Grease and line with parchment paper three 18cm round cake tins.
Combine all the sauce ingredients and slowly stir in a bowl over a pan of gently simmering water until melted together. To make the cake, place the butter, sugar into a food mixer or bowl with an electric handheld mixer. Add eggs, then add the oil, milk and vanilla extract. Sieve the flour and cocoa together, mix with the rest of the ingredients. Add 5 tbps of the chocolate fudge sauce. Mix until all the ingredients have combined well and the mixture is smooth. Divide the cake batter between the prepared tins. Bake in the oven for 30–40 mins. When the cake springs back to the touch place on cooling racks. When still slightly warm spoon a couple of tablespoons of the fudge sauce onto the upturned bottoms. These will become the middles which will be sandwiched together. Leave to cool.
Prepare a creamy butter icing by combining the butter and sieved icing sugar creaming together until smooth. Add the vanilla essence. Spoon a little butter icing onto one of the cakes then place another cake on top. Repeat. Ice the top of the cake with more butter icing (you can pipe it if you want a fancy effect) Garnish with chocolate shards and dribbles of the fudge sauce. Enjoy.

Chris Coleman

Island Brewery
Shalfleet

I've been brewing beer commercially for over two decades, and started working as Head Brewer for the Island Brewery eight years ago. Together with Tom Minshull and his son Steve, I helped set the brewery up, overseeing the conversion of the industrial site we're based at, and travelling all over the country to source cutting edge brewing equipment. There's a rich tradition of brewing on the Island, and we're proud to continue that tradition as a family-run company. I've taken a step back from the day-to-day brewing now, and my son Ashley runs that side of things.

We currently brew seven different real ales, five of which – Wight Gold, Yachtsman's Ale, Nipper Bitter, Vectis Venom and Wight Knight – date from the day we started in 2010. Our cask beers are sold to pubs across the Isle of Wight and all along the South coast, while our bottled beers are sold in local farm shops and served on the Wightlink ferry. In 2013 we introduced another beer, Wight Christmas, which won a prestigious Gold in the 2015 World Beer Awards. Our Earl's Rich Dark Ale was brewed with the Hospice in mind (they receive 10p from every pint we sell) and it has won CAMRA's Beer of the Year for the last three years – it tastes superb in a beef stew too! I couldn't have favourites, but our best-seller is the Yachtsman's Ale which is a nice blend of darker ale, moderately hoppy, and seems to satisfy quite a few different taste palettes – yachtsmen and landlubbers alike!

Our secret is all down to having the best equipment, knowledgable staff, and a total commitment to quality ingredients. It's not the cheapest way to make something, but if you cut corners and produce an inferior product, people aren't going to buy it anyway! So if you have to charge a little bit more to produce a top class beer then that's what you have to do!

The Island is a special place. Everybody knows everybody really, and if you do a good job of things you get local feedback fairly quickly. Luckily we've always had a very positive response to all our beers, so we must be doing something right!

Wight Gold Chocolate Cake

Island Brewery
Shalfleet

For 8

200ml Wight Gold, plus 4 tbsp for the icing
50g cocoa powder/drinking chocolate
110g Briddlesford butter, softened
275g soft light brown sugar
2 large Isle of Wight free-range eggs
175g Calbourne Mill self-raising flour
2 tbsp condensed milk
1 tsp vanilla paste
220g Seaforth chocolate
220g icing sugar
100g soft Briddlesford butter

Grease and flour two 18cm cake tins.

Preheat the oven to 180°C / Gas Mark 4.

Slowly mix the Wight Gold into the cocoa powder to form a paste.

In a separate bowl, beat the butter and soft brown sugar together until smooth and creamy, then add the eggs one at a time beating between each addition.

Stir in the cocoa and ale mixture. Sift in the flour, in batches, stirring between each addition. Add the condensed milk and vanilla paste and mix well.

Pour the cake batter into the prepared tins and bake for 30–35 minutes, or until springy to the touch. Cool on a wire rack.

Melt the chocolate in a heatproof bowl suspended over a pan of simmering water.

Beat the icing sugar and butter together to form a soft paste. Add four tablespoons of Wight Gold and then fold in the melted chocolate.

Sandwich the two cakes together with the beer and chocolate icing.

Serve with a dust of icing sugar over the top of the cake.

Jackie Carder

Mottistone Farm
Hulverstone

Now that our son has joined us on the farm, he has become the fourth generation of farmers in the family. It's very much a family business – we do all the work ourselves along with a young lad who works for us part time. He came to us as an apprentice from Sparsholt College a few years ago and splits his time between us and one other local farm.

We have farmed at Hulverstone for 27 years, then 12 years ago the tenancy for the neighbouring farm at Mottistone became available from its owners, the National Trust. We applied straight away as we wanted to expand. We were so pleased when we were granted the tenancy as it made perfect sense for us.

Together, the farms at Mottistone, Tennyson, Ventnor and St Catherine's amount to approximately 1,000 acres. Although they are two separate farms we see them as one enterprise and all our meat is branded as Mottistone Farm. We farm beef, lamb and pigs with some arable land, too.

We live in a very special landscape. Many of our fields are on chalk downs and much of our grazing land is coastal so the lamb, in particular, has a sweet, intense taste that comes from the salt winds. It's a very different taste to lamb grown inland and it makes for deliciously flavoured meat.

We believe that our animals should have plenty of room and that's another aspect that gives our meat such a special flavour. It's the opposite of intensive farming.

We produce three flavours of pork sausages – a slightly spicy Traditional Old English recipe, a Rare Breed flavour and our special Jubilee recipe which we introduced to celebrate the Queen's Diamond Jubilee in 2012. The sausages are flavoured with a blend of nutmeg, cinnamon and sage and proved so popular that we're still making them five years on.

You can find our meat in some local pubs but if you want to cook it yourself at home, then go to Brighstone Village Shop or Yarmouth Deli. Both shops sell a great range of Mottistone Farm products. You can also buy it direct from me.

Jubilee Sausages with Celeriac Mash and Onion and Ale Gravy

Mottistone Farm

Hulverstone

For 4

1 celeriac – peeled, cut into chunks
1kg floury potatoes – peeled, cut into chunks
150g butter plus extra for the gravy
Salt and freshly ground black pepper
1 large onion
2 tbsp of Oil of Wight plus a little more for frying the sausages
1 tbsp of tomato puree
1 tsp sugar
1 tbsp Calbourne plain flour
425ml of Yachtman's Ale
8 Jubilee pork sausages

Boil the potatoes in a large pan of salted boiling water for 20–25 mins until tender, adding the celeriac after about 5 mins. Drain and mash well with a potato masher in the dry pan. Add the butter , season with salt and black pepper. Keep covered and warm.

While the potatoes and celeriac are cooking, peel, halve and thinly slice the onion lengthways into semicircles. Heat the oil in a heavy bottomed frying pan and cook the onions on a medium heat until soft and lightly coloured. Add the tomato puree, sugar and flour to thicken. Stir for a minute or two before slowly adding the Ale.

Fry the sausages in a frying pan with a little oil. Cook until golden brown and the juices run clear.

Whisk a knob of butter into the gravy to thicken it slightly. To serve, divide the mash between four plates, place two sausages on each dollop of mash and pour the ale gravy over it.

Mary Case

Limerstone

I was born and brought up on the Island. I'm the daughter of a farmer and I'm married to a farmer. In 1984 I attended a beekeeping course at Sparsholt College and I've been hooked on beekeeping ever since, initially as a hobby but over time it has grown into a thriving business. I love encouraging customers to try different types of honey. I sell them on my market stall at the weekly Island Farmer's Market, held in St Thomas' Square, Newport, of which I'm one of the original founders.

Each batch of honey tastes different, depending on which apiary it was collected from. The taste also depends on the flora available to the hives and at which point in the beekeeping season it was harvested.

Honey is best eaten on warm toast. Late season honey tends to be stronger whilst early oil seed rape honey will set hard with a mild taste. I sell clear and set honey in several different size jars and cut comb.

Luckily the Island is one of the sunniest places in the UK. Beekeeping is reliant on the weather, without warm sunny weather there will be no nectar for the bees to collect. The majority of my hives are made of high-density polystyrene. Compared to wooden hives, polystyrene is warmer and drier in the winter and cooler in the summer.

I love to encourage and demonstrate beekeeping to those wishing to take up the craft. During my 30 years of beekeeping I've hosted many beekeeping visits to my apiaries.

I also have an orchard behind my house in Limerstone. It's stocked with 25 different varieties of apple trees, including Blenheim Orange and Ashmead's Kernel, and from August to December, you can buy our apples from my stall, along with my honey.

In 2013 I had the honour of being the High Sheriff of the Island. I visited many organisations and charities and met lots of interesting and dedicated islanders.

The food scene on the Island excites me. Farmers here have had to re-think how they sell their produce and selling directly to the public has been a big success. Consumers these days want to talk to the producers, they want to know where their food comes from.

Honey Salad Dressing

Mary Case Honey
Limerstone

I'm not a fan of cooked honey, the heat makes it taste of caramel. I prefer to use honey in a salad dressing or ice cream.

In a jam jar combine

3 tbsp olive oil
3 tbsp sunflower oil
3 tbsp rice vinegar or white wine vinegar
16 tbsp clear honey
1 dessert spoon Dijon or English mustard

This is the basic recipe to which you can add some of the following
A crushed anchovy fillet
Teasp finely chopped thyme
A crushed clove of garlic
Teasp whole grain mustard
Glug of Worcester sauce

Shake well and enjoy!

Round the Island Race

Michelle Stevens

Bouldnor

Moving to the Isle of Wight in the summer of 2013 is possibly one of the best things we have ever done. We always loved the natural beauty here and the fact that the local produce scene is so strong. My husband Richard and I initially opened a shop on the High Street in Yarmouth, and found the town to be extremely welcoming.

By 2015, we were ready to fully open The Green Barn in Bouldnor.

Our farm is the first, and only, commercial dairy goat farm on the Island. Here, we produce a range of both plain and flavoured soft goat's cheese including garlic and mixed herb.

Our selection of products also includes traditional crumbly goat's milk fudge in a variety of flavours, as well as freshly-bottled pasteurised goat's milk. New in 2018, we started producing a new cheese – Rind Ripening Goat's Cheese. It has a firmer texture with a bloomy white rind – it's flavours changing and developing over the life of the cheese.

We are proud to be able to supply many of the local farm shops across the Island as well as a number of restaurants and chefs, notably Robert Thompson of Thompson's in Newport. Goats have been a part of our lives for as long as I can remember. We moved our small herd over with us from Windsor. Today we have a 60-strong herd of mainly British Saanen, with Golden Guernseys and British Toggenburgs increasingly featuring too. Although a little picky about the weather, our herd are free to graze outside all year.

Within our herd, we have three generations all milking, and our highest yielding goat was Tink, who gave us an amazing 9.6 litres of milk a day at her peak!

Ours is a true family business. Although pursuing their own careers, our daughter Eleanor and son Josh are also actively involved in many of the aspects of the day-to-day running of the farm and business.

At the farm, we openly invite visitors to come and meet our goats (as well as us!). We stock a range of local produce in our farm shop alongside antique prints and crafts from local artists, and offer tea and coffee – using our fresh goat's milk, of course!

Goat's Cheese Whirls

The Green Barn
Bouldnor

Goat's Cheese is an incredibly versatile product. Whether you fancy a quick bite, a main meal, or an indulgent dessert, the scope for use is endless – being enjoyed as an ingredient within a dish, or simply on its own.

Quick to whip up, these are the perfect nibble for any party – and they can be easily tweaked for your guests too. Instead of mustard, try some fresh or dried herbs to give it a little kick – or you could even substitute the Tomato Relish for Marmite!

Should there be any going spare, they also make for a perfect light accompaniment to a crispy salad.

> Makes: 12-15
>> 175g Calbourne plain flour
>> 1 tsp mustard
>> 50g butter
>> 50g goat's cheese
>> 1 Isle of Wight free-range egg
>> Isle of Wight tomato relish
>> Goat's milk – for brushing

Preheat oven to 180°C / Gas Mark 4. Grease two baking trays.
Sift the flour into a bowl, rubbing in the mustard and butter to form breadcrumbs. Add in the goat's cheese. Mix well before gradually adding in enough beaten egg to form a firm dough. Roll out the dough into an inch thick oblong. Evenly spread with tomato relish and roll up firmly – like a Swiss Roll.
Cut into thick slices and place on a baking tray, lightly brushing the top surface with goat's milk. Bake until pale golden in colour and firm to touch – roughly 20–25 mins.
Allow to cool, serve, and enjoy.

Neal Smith

Calbourne Water Mill
Calbourne

I trained as a Millwright and started working at Calbourne Water Mill when it came back into production in 1982. Calbourne Water Mill is the only working water mill on the Isle of Wight and, at over 1000 years old, is one of the oldest working water mills in the country, dating right back to the Domesday Book.

I've been here 35 years now. I work with my brother Mike; you can work the Mill alone but if there are visitors then you need two people. We're milling every day of the week, except Saturdays and visitors can come and watch the process daily at 3 pm during the summer season.

We are proud that our flour is ground the 'traditional way', using only the power of water, and we produce approximately 120 tons of flour and oats each year. My favourite flour is the Calbourne White wheatmeal – it's got a rise like a white flour but is nutritionally closer to a wholemeal. This is what the big bakers are using these days and are selling as 50/50, 'good for you' healthy loaves.

We produce 18 different flours – including an organic range, and 14 oat-based porridges and mueslis. We buy our grain locally where we can or from the mainland, depending on what we can get in the harvest conditions of that year. We then mill the grain to produce wholemeals, two types; a fine wholemeal and a wholemeal with a large bran flake. The wholemeal large flake we can sieve or dress to leave us with a white flour, semolina, bran, and the wheatmeal flour which we sell as Calbourne White.

We also do spelt and rye. Spelt flour can replace wheat flour anywhere you want really – it's got a more earthy, nutty flavour. It's an ancient grain and doesn't crop very heavily so it's more expensive. It's high in gluten but the gluten protein is different to that in our modern wheat, so many people that can't eat modern wheat are still able to eat spelt.

All our non-organic flours come from the Island, but as we don't have an organic wheat producer here on the Island our grain has to come from the mainland. We started doing oats again in 2006; previously we only did oatmeal off the mill stone. We buy groats and then either roll them to make porridge oats or muesli oats.

Our products are available across the Island in Co-ops, independent food and farm shops. We also deliver to the mainland and sell flour direct through our online shop.

Calbourne Water Mill Flapjacks

Calbourne Water Mill

Calbourne

For 8

    300g unsalted butter
    75g demerara sugar
    120g golden syrup (6 tbsps)
    250g Calbourne Mill porridge oats
    250g Calbourne Mill jumbo rolled oats

Line a 30 x 20cm baking tray with baking parchment.
Preheat the oven to 180°C / Gas Mark 4.
Place the butter, sugar and syrup into a saucepan and melt the ingredients, stirring constantly until liquid. Do not boil!
Take off the heat. Blend the oats together and stir into the liquid mixture.
Once mixed then place onto the prepared baking tray and spread evenly.
Bake for 25–30 mins.
Allow to cool but before the flapjack sets, cut into the required portions.
Mixed fruit or nuts can be added to this recipe at the oats addition stage.

Freshwater

Caroline Gurney-Champion

I was born on the Island and, after doing my A levels at Carisbrooke, I skipped up to London vowing never to return. But return I did after a career as a film producer – the pull of the sea was too great. My four children were brought up and educated on the Isle of Wight and when the youngest was very small I started B&B at Gotten Manor in Chale. The business has expanded to include three holiday cottages.I am really lucky to live in such a beautiful place, I feel grounded in the earth and know that especially when I am on Compton beach that I am conscious of the generations of my family who have been here before me. It's a humbling realisation.

Fred Smith

I was born in Brook on the south coast and it remains my favourite part of the Island. I went to school at West Wight and Carisbrooke High School but really grew up spending every day I could playing cricket for Ventnor at Steephill Cove. After studying in Nottingham I co-founded graphic design agency Smith and Agar in 2009 specifically working on prints and branding for the fashion industry. I now live in London with my wife and two young children and I still miss the summers, beaches and particularly the cricket club.

Photographers' Profiles

Julian Winslow
I've been a freelance photographer for 13 years. That path was born out of love for the creative process and the medium. I get a lot of pleasure from collaborating with people who are passionate about what they do and this project has been full of those people. I'm really grateful to be given the opportunity to give something back to the hospice who have supported family and friends of mine at the most difficult times with grace and empathy. Thank you.

Cam Snudden is a serial creative born on the Isle of Wight. Sculpting, drawing, graphic design, music and photography are some of the directions and modalities where that creativity has found its way into the public arena. That energy is now concentrated in photography though if you find him at home he'll probably have a guitar in his hand.

Available Light Photography is the landscape work of myself, **Steve Gascoigne.** Having started my career in photo-journalism 25 years ago, I moved into darkroom printing and colour management where I learnt the art of producing finely crafted images for some of the country's leading photographers. A visit to the Island in the winter of 1999 made me realise that slaving away in a darkroom all day was no longer for me – I wanted to be outdoors! So less than a year later my wife Sharon and I made the move to the Island and began photographing the beautiful and diverse landscape that is the Isle of Wight. I am now privileged enough to earn my living doing what I love.

Fiona Sims skips the globe in pursuit of top chefs, pioneering food producers, hot hotels and legendary winemakers. She writes about her experiences for a number of magazines and newspapers, including *The Times, The Sunday Times, Food & Travel* and *Decanter*. She is also the author of four books, including *The Boat Cookbook* (Bloomsbury), and her latest, *The Boat Drinks Book*, also published by Bloomsbury, and she is the editor of Island Visitor magazine.

Debbie Pentelow is a freelance journalist with more than 20 years' experience in corporate communications. She swapped London for the Isle of Wight in 2011 and now lives in Freshwater. Debbie also works part-time at the West Wight Medical Practice in Freshwater.

Alix Robinson is a wordsmith who set up home on the Isle of Wight after falling in love with it (and a sailor) many years ago. She lives here with said sailor, two daughters, one dog and her horse. With a history in travel and food PR and journalism, Alix is currently editor of myIsleofWight.com, online magazine and *Independent Guide to the Island*, which shares authentic local Islanders' knowledge through features, guides and blogs. Prior to that she worked with Island producers and across the Island food sector as the editor of the original, now deceased, *Taste of the Wight Magazine*.

Anna Pocock spent ten years making television programmes, before moving to the Isle of Wight to raise her family. She now writes content and produces marketing videos for both local businesses and national magazines. www.islewrite.wordpress.com

Lindsay Becker is the editor of *Taste of the Wight*, the Island's leading local food and drink guide. She also regularly contributes to *Wightlife* magazine. Born and bred on the Island, Lindsay can regularly be found out and about on the beautiful isle, maybe paddle-boarding, maybe walking, but more than likely eating. A lover of all things 'Wight', Lindsay believes there is no greater place to live and work than here.

Sarah Sims launched Copy Inc. to help businesses tell their story. After years of working in the national media as journalist and feature writer, she now works across all platforms as a brand strategist for digital content, print and editorial, PR and social media. She creates carefully-crafted, branded copy and content on any subject, across all industry sectors to give businesses the right voice to communicate effectively with their customers. She works for organisations nationwide and for local businesses on the Isle of Wight to strengthen their brand positioning in the marketplace.

Potters' Profiles

Molly Attrill was born on the Island. She was apprenticed to Michael Leach in North Devon, then studied ceramics at the West Surrey College of Art (Farnham) from 1974 to 1977. She worked in France and Canada as a journeyman potter before returning to the Island and establishing her pottery at Mersley Farm in 1982. Since 2014 she has been based at Binnel Studios, St Lawrence. Molly makes attractive pots for everyday use.

Sue Paraskeva has worked with porcelain and other clays for over 25 years and was resident artist at Jubilee Stores where she taught ceramics until 2013. She continues to develop a multi-faceted practice which combines tableware, one-off pieces and installation work, using traditional techniques of thrown and altered porcelain firing in a gas kiln. She is evolving her visual language by altering fine porcelain vessels through the performative actions of smashing, dropping or throwing. The process is highly individual and adds resonance to the direction of work by establishing a vocabulary through which to explore social and domestic issues. Her ongoing interest in both the process and outcomes achieved through working in this way has led to live and recorded performances becoming an integral part of her practice – including live performances at Collect 2017 at the Saatchi Gallery among others.

An NHS public art commission has also helped enable over 10,000 people a year to engage therapeutically with craft via a permanent installation of porcelain wall pieces at Ryde Community Clinic. She continues to supply Calvin Klein Home, New York, with the 'Quay' porcelain tableware range and one-off plates to the 2* Michelin chef Tom Kerridge.

Neil Tregear was born in 1959. He started making pottery at high school in San Francisco and continued his training with a degree in Ceramics from Middlesex Polytechnic, followed by an apprenticeship with Yamada Hikaru in Kyoto, Japan. His first studio was in Oxford. As well as producing his own work for shops such as Libertys and Primavera, he has collaborated with Isis Ceramics producing Delft ware that was widely exported. He moved to the Isle of Wight in 2003.

"My wonderful studio is based in the old butcher's shop in Niton. I currently employ a small team designing and making our own unique style of decorative stoneware pottery. Our work is sold and exhibited extensively across the UK. It has also featured in major exhibitions in Paris and Tokyo. The Isle of Wight continues to provide an excellent base for my work."

The Hospitality and Catering Department at the Isle of Wight College

At the Isle of Wight College, the Hospitality department is one of the busiest. We are proud to train and support the young Island talents of the future in our facilities, as well as helping many local charities. We are involved in various events throughout the year, such as weddings, banquets, local charity fundraisers, as well as working alongside employers with our apprentice's scheme. We are here to train and support young Islanders, and help them develop life skills, numeracy and literacy, improving communication and raising self-confidence. Our mission is to support all students and continue to raise aspirations in the local community.

The Hospitality Team
Emmanual Ferdinand
Clair Etchell-Johnson

Students
Joshua Abbott
Morgan Lacey
Luca Speight
Zak Hamilton-Toogood
Alan McCall

General Index

Index of Recipes

Acknowledgements

This has been an amazing experience.

I would just like to say a big big special thank you to all the wonderful people who helped with this book. You all know who you are. It has been a real privilege and delight to experience the new (and old) talent on the Isle of Wight. We have it in abundance. Everyone has been extraordinarily magnanimous with their time.

I want to thank Peter Harrigan for approaching me to be project manager, for giving me the freedom to progress this book as I liked and for his constant encouragement in phone calls, walks, meals, and generously allowing me into his life.

Also thanks to Emma Topping at Earl Mountbattan Hospice for support and ideas in promoting the book on the Isle of Wight and her colleague Tina Groves for coordinating the project with the Hospice and its CEO.

Also to Krissi Hill also at Medina for her marketing knowledge and for promoting Nammet beyond the Isle of Wight.

Ginormous hugs, and whopping respect . . .

To Julian Winslow and Cam Snudden for their amazing photography and for making hectic shoot days fun; and to Simon Wells for letting us use his studio and for making boundless cups of tea and coffee.

To Fiona Sims for finding and briefing a bevy of Island writers who all came in with their producer profiles before the deadline.

To the students and tutors in the Catering department at the IW College. How you managed to test and cook – all 34 recipes in two days I will never know. I take my hat off to you all. A seriously major achievement.

To Paul Jennings for tirelessly and patiently helping me with laptop issues -my skills are rubbish - what would I have done without you Paul?

To Mary Wilson for pointing out all my errors and being a scrupulous proof reader.

And especially to Fred Smith for his tireless work in designing a beautiful book, being my rock and for putting up with my endless questions, texts and facetime calls all hours of the day and night.

Thank you

Caroline Gurney-Champion